creative ESSENTIALS

Nathan Parker

SHORT FILMS

...how to make and distribute them

creative ESSENTIALS

This edition published in 2007 by Kamera Books
PO Box 394, Harpenden, Herts, AL5 1XJ
www.kamerabooks.co.uk

Copyright © Nathan Parker 2007
Series Editor: Hannah Patterson

A CIP catalogue record for this book is available from the British Library.

ISBN-10: 1-904048-81-1
ISBN-13: 978-1-904048-81-7

Typeset by Elsa Mathern
Printed by SNP Lefung Printers (Shenzen) Co Ltd, China

CONTENTS

INTRODUCTION

With a history as long as cinema itself, the short film is a vital format. It provides the opportunity for the filmmaker to experiment and learn in equal measure. Although most filmmakers long for big budgets and the opportunity to direct a feature-length film, it's easy to forget the artistic and commercial restrictions that come with studio backing; and work dictated by finance rather than creativity often compromises the director's vision. Short filmmaking offers the chance to express yourself without these limitations, the freedom to deal with ideas, subject matter and aesthetics that might be considered either too radical or commonplace for features.

Whether you are planning on making a 15-second video piece or a 30-minute drama on 35mm, you will be dealing with the same principles and processes of filmmaking. You may intend to make a short either as a chance to experiment or as a stepping-stone to feature directing, but the process of producing it will give you invaluable first-hand experience and also the potential to influence and inspire others through your film.

Due to technological advances, filmmaking is no longer a medium reserved for professionals. With the ever-increasing quality of domestic cameras and computer-based editing systems, it's now possible to create a film with a high-end look for very little. With the accessibility and quality of this equipment, more and more people are now becoming involved in short filmmaking. As a result, there are more places to screen your film once it's made, whether through Internet streaming, or at one of the many worldwide film festivals.

While it's a great time to be making short films, the journey can be perilous. There are endless choices to be made at every stage, from formats, through casting to distribution. If you aren't armed with the right knowledge, it's easy to become unstuck along the way. Many potential filmmakers find the process daunting, and this can lead to unfinished films or shorts that, once made, simply never get seen. This book is designed to help you to overcome these hurdles and facilitate the entire short filmmaking process, giving you insight into the options available to you, and helping you find the right route for your film; from the initial idea to the moment when an audience finally watches it on the screen.

CONTEXT

Although the first films ever made were short in nature, the longer-duration format – or feature film – evolved quickly. Traditionally, filmmaking has belonged to large film studios that generated their monopoly on cinema through commercial productions, with feature-length films their most financially viable products. Due to its lack of commercial viability, short film has almost exclusively existed as an independent art form, often the only type of filmmaking available to people unconnected to or backed by large studios.

Short film's independent nature has ensured it as a fertile area of innovation and experimentation, at the cutting edge of film, both technically and ideologically. Unhindered by more conservative studio systems, shorts have really been the breeding ground for many of the ideas and approaches that have then been re-absorbed into features. Short filmmaking therefore provides you with an opportunity to influence the way that films are made and how they look, as well as audiences and other filmmakers. Just one short film – Maya Deren's experimental *Meshes of the Afternoon* for example – is capable of redefining how people perceive films and cinema in general.

EXPERIENCE

At the beginning of your filmmaking process you need to build enough knowledge of all the different elements that go into creating a complete film. This does not mean reading every book and manual on the subject. While books on filmmaking are a valuable resource, filmmaking cannot be learned theoretically. Although it requires meticulous planning and coordination, it also relies on intuition, creativity and experience. The real learning process occurs when you put your ideas into practice. It's only by getting out there and making your own films, or helping others to make theirs, that you will begin to gain a thorough understanding of how films are really made. It's this experience that will ultimately help you develop a sense for filmmaking and allow you to hone your skills.

If you are a novice filmmaker you may strive for perfection, but you'll learn a great deal through your mistakes. The disappointment you may feel when your film on screen doesn't match up with your original vision shouldn't discourage, but rather inspire you. You can use what you have learned to make your next project better, and it's largely through this process that you will develop into a skilful and well-rounded filmmaker.

SKILLS

Filmmaking by its very nature doesn't depend on the talent of just one person, and what makes a good film is a unique combination of skilled people. The most important skill that you need as a director, or filmmaker, is the ability to communicate your vision to other people, not just with your finished film but to those involved in the process of making it. Whether it's with an actor, cinematographer or composer, you will need to communicate clearly what you have in mind and what you require of them to make your ideas possible. For this you need to develop specific communication skills and learn the languages of filmmaking. Each filmmaking discipline has its own specific terminology and mode of expression. Explaining to an actor what emotion you would like them to manifest is very different to explaining to a Director of Photography (DP) how you would like a shot to be framed and lit. One of the key purposes of this book is to explain the languages of the different roles involved in filmmaking and help you to communicate your ideas.

WHAT YOU WILL GET OUT OF THIS BOOK

These days short film is an ubiquitous art form. You can make one on your phone in 20 seconds, have it on the net in a few minutes and potentially broadcast it to millions on *YOUTUBE* in a matter of days. This book, however, is designed for people that want to push their ideas and skills towards more complex productions. Creating short films that are well-thought out, well-crafted and well-executed.

This book is designed to cover the majority of technical aspects and options involved in completing a short film. It should provide you with a comprehensive overview that will allow you to choose from a range of established methods and techniques to create your own unique film. Although these methods are based on conventional filmmaking practices, the films you make don't have to be. It merely provides a structure within which you can create your own vision. Subjects such as cinematography or scriptwriting are discussed but for more in-depth treatment you would be wise to look elsewhere.

Aside from an all-round practical and theoretical knowledge, a range of interviews also offers you the opportunity to observe how other filmmakers have created their films and on the accompanying DVD are the results of their experiences.

1. TURNING YOUR IDEA INTO A FILM

Although there is no one filmmaking formula, there are many established filmmaking methods, some of which have evolved from the feature film industry and are often adapted and downsized for the purposes of short filmmaking.

Although a number may not apply to small-budget short films, several are extremely useful if not essential in planning and shooting a short of any length or budget.

Filmmaking protocol is of course always in flux. Established methods can suddenly become obsolete with the advent of a new piece of technology. Even well-established conventions are constantly being modified and tailored to suit the needs of an individual film. Most feature filmmaking methods have come about in order to make the process of production more efficient and minimise the potential for problems.

The result is a series of tried and tested methods, which are practiced in all areas of filmmaking. They aren't rules as such, and no one is going to insist you adhere to them, but there is a great deal to be learned from the experiences of thousands of other filmmakers.

The methods described in this book are derived from established techniques. While films vary in style, content and duration, making it practically impossible to follow a specific model from start to finish, having a good understanding of conventional practices allows you to pick and choose which ones work best for you. For this, you will need to evaluate the specific needs of your film and work through a process of elimination to determine which are most applicable to your short. Ultimately they are designed to help you make your film with greater ease.

DEVELOPING YOUR IDEA

The concept for a short film can come from anywhere. There are no rules about what makes for good subject matter, no rules about the way in which you present it to an audience; both can be as direct or abstract as you want. While this freedom is short filmmaking's obvious appeal, it can sometimes be overwhelming.

One of the most useful strategies for finding and developing ideas is to work out what limitations you will face during the creation of your film. The key to turning a good idea into a good film is to work within your means and you should carefully evaluate your potential ideas in light of the following considerations:

BUDGET

Although short filmmaking is a chance to let your imagination manifest itself on screen, more often than not you will find that imagination can be very expensive in practical terms.

Generally the main limitation when making shorts is budget. The budget – or lack of it – will dictate what kinds of ideas you can develop and eventually realise. Large casts and elaborate sets are expensive to incorporate; and while you should aim high with your overall production values, you need to be realistic to achieve optimum results within the boundaries of your budget.

DURATION

Short films can range from a few seconds to 30 minutes. You don't have to squeeze your action into one minute or five, but can create a bespoke length, developing an appropriate pace and rhythm over an unspecified period. This means you can explore topics or events that would seldom sustain a feature-length film or follow more common structures; and this is something that you should try and use to your advantage.

When choosing a subject, try and think about a topic that lends itself to both the medium of film and the duration of a short. For instance, unlike a feature, you often don't have much time to develop plots or characters. Trying to compress a significant amount of either can thus prove both futile and impossible. Shorts that attempt to shoehorn too much material can seem chaotic and leave an audience confused. Faced with a blank page, it's tempting to work with an abundance of ideas, but it's important as your film develops to eliminate anything extraneous and really focus in on what it is you're trying to say.

TIME

The experience of watching a film is designed to be deceptive: the audience should remain unaware of the effort that goes into a production, which makes it easy to forget just how much time and energy is really involved.

You therefore need to consider not just how much time you can devote to the project, but also how much you can expect other people to give. The film will be a passion for you and hopefully this enthusiasm will be infectious enough to attract people to the project, but you have to be realistic about their commitments, particularly in terms of your budget.

DON'T LET YOUR IDEAS GO TO WASTE

Given the chance, most filmmakers would of course welcome a large budget, professional crew and talented cast, but only a few are ever given access to all these components; and the chances are they didn't start out with them.

Your ideal story may be set on an alien space station or in the 16th century, but rather than shelve these ideas until a big budget materialises, knowing your limitations can actually help you turn your ideas into films. Try and locate what it is about these particular topics/situations that interests you, and then devise more unusual ways in which you can make them work within other, more feasible contexts.

Many successful short films are created from the most basic premise, and the simplest of ideas can be turned into extremely complex films; complex as a viewing experience doesn't necessarily mean complex to make.

2. SCRIPTING

TREATMENT

A treatment is the name for a written outline of your film. More in depth than a synopsis but less precise than a script, it can range from a few lines to a few pages. It is designed to inform people of the film's key elements and how they would play out. It should be easily readable and give people an idea of what your film will be like when it's finished. Unlike a script, which often has a standard format and structure, a treatment can take the written form that most suits the material of the film.

DO YOU NEED A SCRIPT?

Many short film ideas may either have little dialogue or be purely visual. Creating a script may not be necessary. You might be able to convey your idea much more clearly with a fully drawn storyboard, or even a few sketches. However, creating a script, even if it is only a few lines long, or merely a list of directions, can often be very useful.

A script is essentially a reference tool for everyone involved in the making of the film and will often be necessary for much of the film's pre-production. For instance, a casting director, or auditioning actor, will normally need to see a script in order to understand the nature of the project and what will be required of them. While on the shoot a script will allow both cast and crew to keep a track of the context of a certain scene and its direction. It provides a single point of reference for everybody, giving directorial information for actors and director, or technical information for a DP and sound recordist.

The process of turning an idea into a script also allows you to break the material down into its individual elements. Whether this is lines of dialogue, directions or actions, in doing this you will be better able to reshape and refine the structure of your idea.

FORMATTED SCRIPTS

With feature films, a script or screenplay needs to obey a specific style universally used throughout the film industry. Feature film scripts often exist for years before they ever get made and will be read by hundreds of people, hence the necessity of a generic format. With short films, however, where the process is often more immediate, it is not necessary to format your script in such a conventional manner. For people that think their film requires or would benefit from a formatted script, there is a huge variety of script formatting software available, the most widely used being *Final Draft*. http://www.finaldraft.com

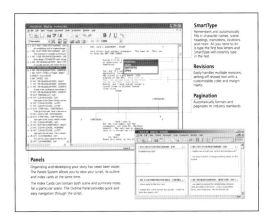

Figure 1. *Final Draft* scriptwriting programme. www.finaldraft.com

3. STORYBOARDING

Storyboarding is one of the most important elements in the short filmmaking process. While a lot of feature-length films rely strongly on scripted dialogue and character development to drive the film, with short films the emphasis is often on the visual, with many films having no dialogue at all. In this last case in particular, the storyboard provides the keystone to the entire production.

The storyboard is the place where you first begin to visualise your film, to see how the shots and moves will work together to create the whole.

WHAT STORYBOARDS LOOK LIKE

Essentially the storyboard will resemble a comic strip version of your film. It will consist of a series of sequential images that shows each of the different shots. A good storyboard is often the key to a good film.

When you are storyboarding, you are not only working out what you want to shoot but also providing a reference for everyone else involved in the production. It will give the art department instant information about what they will need for the overall film, as well as the specifics of individual scenes. It will provide the DP the first concrete insight of your ideas for framing and lighting, as well as camera moves. It will also be a resource for the actors, and help them to see what kind of action they will be expected to take.

Whether your film has no conventional narrative, is only ten seconds long or has no script, storyboarding really is worth taking the time over. It's often through the process of creating the storyboard that you will first encounter the practical problems in shooting a scene – an impossible camera angle, for instance, or the logistics of having too many people in one room.

The storyboard is also a great place to experiment and see how you can make your film visually interesting and innovative. It's the perfect place to try things out, then simply erase and start again. By the time you are on set, it's often too late to start experimenting due to restrictions of time and budget. And if you do have the chance to improvise on set, it is usually because your shoot has been well-planned by adhering to your storyboard.

DIFFERENT STORYBOARDING METHODS

Hand drawn

Even if you are not a talented draughtsman, sitting down with a blank story-board and a pencil is still one of the best methods of working out your ideas. Most storyboards for feature films have been undertaken by a professional storyboard artist; often used during the fundraising stages, they have to be

Figure 2. Storyboards from the short film *Bad Channel* by Sunny Kwak.

very slick. For your short, however, this level of finish is probably not necessary. It really doesn't matter if you are drawing basic stick figures or wonky rooms; as long as the drawings are helping you work out where to place the camera, props and actors, then they are good enough. A useful strategy is often to start working on them very basically for yourself and then getting a friend who can draw to do a more accomplished version for the rest of the crew to use. The storyboard itself can either be downloaded from the Internet, normally as a PDF file, or you can draw it out with a ruler. It is important to decide which aspect ratio you are going to shoot your film in before doing this (see aspect ratio section) so that your storyboard frames' dimensions are the same. The storyboard should also have a couple of lines next to each frame for you to write down information about the action taking place, a camera move or relevant piece of dialogue from the script which is not apparent in the drawing. A 16:9 storyboard template can be downloaded from the accompanying DVD.

Storyboarding software

There are currently several storyboarding programmes on the market. They are straightforward to use and you need absolutely no drawing ability to operate them and produce a professional-looking storyboard. They work by giving you a variety of characters that you can drag and drop onto a background as well as props and locations. The basic 2D programmes allow you to easily change the prop and character dimensions as well as orientation. They also give you the choice between a variety of actions that the characters could be performing, so you can generally find something that matches what you need. The 3D programmes have the advantage of being able to change the camera position and lighting once you have placed your characters in an environment, but they are often much more complicated to use. The images you create are then saved onto a page and can be printed off from the computer with any accompanying text. Although these programmes offer a good alternative to hand-drawn storyboards, they can often be expensive, so remember to plan for this in your budget if you are thinking of buying the software. http://www.storyboardartist.com

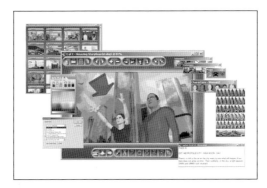

Figure 3. Example of *Storyboard Quick* software.

Photographs and maquettes

Another method is to take a digital stills camera or even a camera phone to the locations that you will be shooting in. This is effective because it enables you to start thinking about the positioning of the camera in the actual location without having to have all the filming equipment there in place. It also enables you to try positioning your actors, or, if they are not available, get friends to stand in for them while you take your pictures. Alternatively you can then load the images onto a computer, print some off and draw your characters directly onto these; you will find that once you've got the real location and camera angle the figures will be much easier to draw. The other option is to build small-scale models of the sets or locations and use anything from articulated wooden figurines to action figures as your characters. Again you can take digital stills and this method will allow you lots of time to experiment.

4. COMPOSITION

Choosing the type of shots that you build your film from occurs both at the storyboarding stage and on the shoot. Creating visually interesting compositions is something that you can do extensively when storyboarding and also on the shoot, either using pencil and paper or a viewfinder. The more thought you put into the composition the more depth and form your film will have.

Depending on the type of equipment you are using to make your film, you will have a variety of options open to you in the composition of each shot. Combining these various options together provides infinite possibilities, so it often helps to break the possible factors down, and work through them one at a time, tweaking each one until you have the desired shot.

CAMERA POSITION (SET UP)

Camera positions are one of the important elements of your shoot. Beyond dictating how your film will look, they also dictate how long your film will take to shoot. Setting up a camera or moving the camera can be a time-consuming process that often entails lighting having to move and change as well. So changing the camera's position as little as possible results in a faster, shorter shoot. However, shooting from a single position or set up does not mean that you will only have one type of shot. By quickly changing lenses, or zooming in and out, you can achieve anything from an extreme close up to an extreme wide shot without ever having to move the camera. Obviously, shooting an entire scene from only one position would give you limited choices, but from two it's possible to create a dynamic variety of shots that can then be intercut in the edit.

Figure 4.
The DP and assistants setting up the shot.

FRAMING

The most natural instinct when framing a shot in a viewfinder is often to cen-tre the subject directly in the middle of the frame. Although effective for some shots, this approach doesn't necessarily create the most dynamic composi-tions. When framing any subject you should always try and make use of the shape of the aspect ratio you have chosen. Dividing the width of the frame up into thirds is a classic technique for making full use of the width of the frame. You can then try and place the subject in alternate thirds.

Figure 5.
A 16:9 widescreen aspect ratio allows for more dynamic framing. Film still from *About a Girl* by Brian Percival.

ANGLE

Once you have decided on a camera position, it is possible to adjust the tripod height and angle, allowing for very different perspectives from a single position. The camera angle can be used to complement the mood of the scene and emphasise the actions or dialogue of a character. For instance high angles can give a sense of vulnerability to an actor, low angles can create an ominous air, while uneven angles can build a sense of unease during a scene. Combining extreme or subtle shifts in angle will subliminally position the viewer where you want them to be, and should be used to help you tell the story.

Figure 6.
Low camera angle, creating a menacing feel. Still from Jan Kounen's *Gisele Kerozene*.

SPEED

Controlling the speed at which the audience sees things is one of the great capabilities of film. The use of slow motion is both a stylistic device and can also control how you deliver action and information. Over-cranking or under-cranking the camera you can achieve combinations of time lapse and slow motion to give your film a rhythm that reflects the material.

Figure 7.
Classic slow motion allowing a prolonging of the moment. Shot by Simon Minett.

COLOUR

Unless you are shooting on black and white, juxtapositions of colour can be used for subtle or spectacular effect. Contemplating the colour scheme of each shot will give you the potential to create a dynamic range that should include costume, props, scenery and lighting. The psychological resonance of certain colours has been widely used in filmmaking, and is as much a tool to create mood or feel as any camera techniques. Choices over film stock and grading can also drastically alter the colour scheme of a film, and should be carefully considered from the outset.

Figure 8.
Contrast created between bright and muted colours. Film still from Stephen Daldry's short film *Eight*.

TYPES OF SHOT

The shots you choose to create your film with and the sequence in which they occur should be governed by what you want the audience to see and how you want them to see it. You need to decide what the viewer's focus is and guide them to that point through a single shot or sequence of shots. This can be manifest overtly or implicitly depending on the style of your directing and the subject matter, but it should always inform the type of shots you choose and how you assemble them.

The following is a list of shot types, the terms for which form part of a common language of filmmaking that is useful when trying to convey your ideas to other people. The shots for your film of course can be endless variations and combinations of these.

Wide shot (WS)
Extreme wide shot (EWS)

Wide shots are conventionally used as establishing shots. They give the viewer more information by revealing as much as possible in the frame (generally taking in a person from the feet to just above the head). Wide shots are perfect for establishing a scene because they give the viewer instant information about location and time. However, they also give the viewer a distant viewpoint; with more to look at they won't necessarily concentrate on the area you might want them to. Extreme wide shots can also be used to place a person within a larger landscape.

Medium shot (MS)

The medium shot is the most ubiquitous, often used for framing one or two people from around the waist to just above the head. It creates an objective viewpoint for the audience whilst also engaging them with what you want them to see. Useful as they are, a film consisting entirely of medium shots may seem flat and dimensionless.

Figure 9.
Typical medium shot from Jean-Luc Godard's short film *Charlotte et Veronique*.

Close up (CU)
Extreme close up (ECU)

Close ups are used to draw the audience's attention to a detail that will often have appeared in a previous medium or wide shot. They can be used to give particular significance to a gesture or reveal a pertinent piece of information. Close ups, especially extreme close ups, are very useful when you want to give something a particular emphasis. Yet they can also be disorientating or overly explicit. Extreme close ups can also be used to draw attention to much smaller details, such as an eye or mouth movement that may not otherwise be obvious in a medium or standard close up.

Figure 10.
Typical close up. Still from Spike Jonze's *How They Got Here*.

Point of view (POV)

A POV is used to create a subjective viewpoint, showing the audience exactly what a character is seeing. This is often achieved by combining a medium shot with an on the shoulder filming technique. It is a particularly effective shot when used in conjunction with static objective viewpoint shots.

Over the shoulder

Over the shoulder, not to be confused with on the shoulder, refers to a shot where the camera is positioned above and behind the actor's shoulder, producing a frame where a profile of the actor's face appears on one edge. It is a common shot that gives the audience a good view of what the actor is

Figure 11.
Typical over the shoulder shot from Roman Polanski's *Chinatown*.

seeing without it being a direct POV shot. Conventionally used in conversations between characters.

Single

A single is a shot of just one character. Used in a scene in which only one character appears, it can also visually build the relationship between two or more characters, bringing the focus to that character whether for a piece of dialogue, or for an action. By editing singles together, you can set the pace and rhythm of a conversation to a greater extent than you can with a two shot, cutting out dead air and making responses faster or slower.

Two shot

Refers to a shot containing two people. Although this is a standard shot that may seem straightforward, the composition of a two shot can hint visually at the relationship between the two people. Through use of camera angle, and the positioning and relative height of the characters, you can lend specific emphasis to the way in which they are interacting.

Reverse

A reverse shot is one that takes the exact opposite angle to that which has just been filmed. For example, shooting the back of a character performing an action would often require the reverse angle (the front of the character) to be filmed as well.

CAMERA MOVES

Camera moves can be used for a variety of reasons, such as following action that you could not capture in a static (locked-off) situation, or to guide the viewer through a scene. The possibility for what type of camera moves you can bring to a shot will depend on the grip equipment you choose. To create controlled multi-axis camera moves, such as tracking shots, you will need specific grip gear. Tracks and dollies, cranes and jibs (see grip) all provide very effective ways of providing movement for a shot. When planning your film, however, you need to consider that complex camera moves are time-consuming both to set up and execute. They often need as much if not more rehearsal to perfect as the action they are capturing.

Even simple camera moves can give your film a sophisticated feel, but if overused as a device, injecting movement into every shot, then the power of key dramatic moments can be diminished. If you are going to employ camera moves in your film, it is important to think about when you use them and what kind would be most effective.

Handheld

Handheld camera work can be an effective form of bringing movement to your shots. The rough jerky movements that can be obtained by putting the camera on your shoulder, or carrying it, is perfect for POV shots. The drawback to hand-held camera moves is that they are generally not fluid or consistent enough for use in other circumstances. Unless they visually form part of the narrative, uncontrolled camera moves can be very distracting for an audience.

Pan and tilt

Panning and tilting are the most basic of controlled camera movements. Most tripods will be capable of swivelling left to right or up and down, but to combine the two and keep the movement constant, you will need a tripod with a fluid head (see grip). The speed at which you pan or tilt should be decided according to the shot. Matching up camera movements of different speeds can be difficult during editing so unless you are intending to create a fluctuation in pace then the speeds need to be relatively similar to cut with.

Tracking shots

Tracking shots are fluid camera moves that allow the camera to travel over a chosen distance and create the illusion that the camera is gliding. They can be achieved in a variety of ways, the most common being a track and dolly (see grip). The camera and operator are mounted on the dolly and the wheels of the dolly slot onto lengths of track that run in straight or curved sections. The dolly is then pushed or pulled along and can be brought to a halt within a section of track before continuing or reversing back the way it came. Tracking shots can often be complex to create. They rely on grips manoeuvring the dolly smoothly and will involve changes in framing and focus that will need to be carefully rehearsed. When performed well and under the right circumstances they can be very impressive. Tracking shots can also be produced with a steadicam (see steadicam) or on a super-tight budget by placing the cameraperson in a wheelchair and pushing them around!

Jib/boom

A jib is a swinging cantilever boom. The camera is attached to the jib at one end while the other is counterbalanced with weights. This then pivots on a central support, allowing the camera to produce smooth horizontal and vertical swoops from various heights. They can range in length and are normally designed for different weights of camera. Unlike a crane, which performs the same type of movement but with the camera operator attached, jibs only support the camera, so the camera needs to be operated remotely.

Steadicam

Steadicam is the trademark name for a camera support system that allows multi-axis camera moves. Steadicam allows the same freedom of movement that you can achieve with handheld camera work, but absorbs the shakes and supports the weight of the camera. This allows you to produce continuous fluid shots while the camera roams about.

Zooms

Zooms are not technically a camera move because the camera remains static. They do, however, produce an illusion of movement that is similar to the gliding in or out of a track and dolly move. With a zoom, the size of the frame is reduced so a wide shot will become a close up, and with a tracking shot the size of the frame remains the same. Controlled zoom moves cannot be produced by hand but by a zoom control unit who can create fluid zooms.

5. PRODUCER

The role of the producer is difficult to define; it's a moniker used to describe many different roles and duties within the filmmaking world. The larger the film the more likely it is that there will be various producers onboard, each dealing with different elements of the production process so that financial, practical and managerial responsibilities are split between them. Short films, however, rarely have either the budget or scale to require or allow more than one producer. He or she will therefore deal with all the production elements.

The producer on a short film is normally the person responsible for coordinating the majority of the practical requirements that go into completing the film. They oversee every phase of the film, working closely with the director on all aspects of its production, from budgeting and script rewrites through to distribution.

As much as the producer will be involved in the creative decisions, their priority will be to keep the film on budget and on time, ensuring that the film actually gets completed. The producer achieves this by assembling a team of people that will work well together and also controlling the circumstances in which the film is made. A comprehensive overview of the entire project allows them to keep the production as efficient as possible and foresee potential troubles before they occur.

PRODUCING

The producer is really the key figure in making any film. The director may have the vision and the skill to create a great film given the means, but without a producer to provide those circumstances, the film would never materialise. If you are considering producing a short film, then it's important to be realistic about what it will entail. Producing can be an enormously stressful task; the completion of the film hinges on your efforts, often right down to the last detail. Spending half a day making phone calls to scaffolding companies, for example, is often the reality of what sounds like a glamorous title. That said, the creativity and spirit of most short films can make all the hard work and stress very rewarding and will give you the opportunity to gain crucial experience of how films of any shape or form are made.

SELF-PRODUCING

It is of course possible to take on the role of both producer and director, but such a combination can be difficult. It is not uncommon for this to happen on short films, but usually due to lack of resources rather than a deliberate choice.

Producing and directing are both very demanding roles, and each requires their own type of focus and dedication. Quite apart from spreading yourself too thin psychologically, to do both is often physically impossible.

Aside from the practical considerations, having someone that knows the project as well if not better than you do will bring a sense of perspective to the production and help keep the energy of the project going.

FINDING A PRODUCER

A large proportion of producing a short is coordinating the right elements for the film's specific needs. Whether it's finding cast and crew or hiring equipment, someone who has previous experience as a producer is going to save huge amounts of time and resources.

Although all films have different production requirements, the producer's is a role where experience really counts. An experienced producer will be able to look at the idea or script and immediately begin to assess the resources you will need to make it. They will have an informed view of what the budget might need to be, how long it would take to make and how many people would need to be involved in the process.

The film industry employs an enormous amount of people in a variety of production roles. Often small cogs in the huge commercial feature machine, they will have valuable knowledge and may be interested in taking on small creative projects. Using film crew databases and directly contacting production companies is your best chance of finding them.

If you can't find a professional producer that is interested in your project, then try and find someone that is looking to get experience in that field; a novice with the right ability and attitude will be an enormous asset to the production.

PRODUCERS' DUTIES

The duties of a producer will vary according to the scale of the film and the experience of the people involved. The following is a breakdown of the phases and duties of most producers on short films, but these are normally shared with the director and other key production members.

Pre-production

- Fundraising
- Script development
- Script breakdown
- Scheduling
- Creating a budget
- Organising auditions
- Sourcing crew
- Booking equipment / Locations
- Preparing call sheets

Production

- Organising call times
- Overseeing all departments
- Monitoring the quality of the footage
- Ensuring the production stays on schedule

Post-production

- Coordinating the workflow
- Overseeing the editing
- Ensuring finished film reaches screening formats
- Coordinating distribution plan

INTERVIEW WITH ADRIAN STURGES (PRODUCER)

Adrian Sturges has a wealth of experience producing both successful feature films and award-winning shorts, having produced over 14 films, including *Hotel Infinity*, which is featured on the accompanying DVD. Adrian also has a whole slate of new films in pre-production.

How did you get involved in producing short films?

I started out assisting an established film producer – Simon Relph – and through him met a writer/director called Rupert Wyatt who had a short film script and some cash to make it. We got on and he asked me to get involved.

How many shorts have you produced?

Eight.

What does your role as producer generally entail on a short film?

It normally touches on pretty much every area – from finding the money to setting the budget to hiring the cast and crew with the director and looking for locations, line producing the shoot, sometimes cooking the lunch (!) and supervising all of the post-production. Then there's the afterlife of the film – often a year or more of festivals to look after.

Do you always use the same methods in producing them, or do different projects require different approaches?

I guess there are certain tenets that are always the same but different projects bring different challenges – *Hotel Infinity* had a shoot in a foreign country, *Get The Picture* needed a war zone creating in East London.

How has your experience of working in the film industry influenced your approach to producing short films?

Working on feature films has given me a lot of incredibly useful contacts but really there is nothing like getting out there and making a short to give you a massive amount of experience.

What kind of skills do you think are essential to be a good producer?

You need to be OK with money and managing people and projects but most of all you need to have a nose for good material and that's a skill you must develop yourself. You particularly need to watch lots of films and maintain a strong interest in what's happening on the business side at all times.

Do you think that the more experience you have, the better you get at producing?

Yes, definitely. I sometimes think that if I knew what was needed to be a good producer at the very beginning I would never have started!

Have you seen a lot of different approaches to directing on the films you have produced?

Yes, although the one thing that unites all the directors I've worked with is a singular drive, an obsession with the details of their projects.

What was it about *Hotel Infinity* that made you want to produce it?

I loved the idea – it was so unusual compared to so many shorts I'd read or seen and I was immediately impressed by Amanda and how much work she'd done on preparing the piece.

How did you set about raising the finances for the film? Was it a long process?

Well, the film needed a certain amount of money (because of the foreign location, sizable cast etc) and we weren't timed well for applying for Cinema Extreme, which was the only public scheme at the time that was funding films made on film at this kind of level. So we went about raising the finance privately through a development scheme. It was successful and we got the money we needed but was a massive amount of work for Amanda and I to tackle. Finally, once we made the film, we applied to the Film Council Completion Fund for money to finish it and the timing there was really good – we just had enough material to apply and then the money came through just when we needed it.

Did you manage to get substantial discounts on hiring gear etc?

Yes, we did.

Was this because it was for a short film rather than a commercial feature film?

As always, companies are really supportive of emerging filmmakers.

Were you involved in a lot of the creative decisions as well as the practical ones?

Amanda and I talked about everything but this was very much her screenplay and her vision and it was my job to be supportive of that.

How much time did you have to put into producing the film?

Really hard to quantify! Looking back at my emails, Amanda first contacted me in March 2003 and we delivered the film in time for Edinburgh (August) 2004. Amanda and I have been supporting the film ever since through its festival life (it's still travelling around). I've worked on other projects at the same time, as all producers do, but it's basically a year and a half's work.

Was it difficult finding and obtaining permission to use such good locations?

Switzerland was surprisingly easy. We had a lead on the town Villars sur Ollon and got in touch with the tourist authority there who were incredibly helpful, as were the local residents. We did one recce and then the shoot. The hotel interior was harder to find, Amanda was after long corridors that could be extended in CGI. We looked at lots of places but ultimately went to Bethnal Green Town Hall, which is a favourite – if expensive – film location.

What did you learn from producing *Hotel Infinity* and in retrospect are there any things that you might have done differently?

I learnt a lot from Amanda and I'm particularly proud of how much we pushed ourselves in terms of getting the best people and companies to work on the project. I can't honestly think of anything I would have done differently, although I'm sure there were mistakes I made that I regretted at the time!

How did *Hotel Infinity* compare to other films you have produced? Was it more or less demanding for you as producer?

They're always different. This one was more demanding in terms of scale and intricacy of the production (things like CGI, subtitling, the foreign shoot). But then I've had other films with really tricky elements so I'm not sure a comparison is that meaningful.

What have you done since producing *Hotel Infinity*?

I've produced a couple of other shorts – Gabrielle Russell's *The Wrong Sea* and Gareth Lewis' *Normal For Norfolk*. I've post-supervised a major feature *Merry Christmas* that was nominated for an Oscar this year. I've co-produced two feature films – *Only Human* and *The Front Line*. And this year have produced a comedy pilot for Working Title called *Cul De Sac* and produced two feature films – *The Baker*, directed by Gareth Lewis, and *Warriors*, the new feature documentary from Marc Singer.

What are your plans for the future?

We have a slate of features in development of which Rupert Wyatt's *The Escapist* is due to go into production in January.

What advice would you give to people considering producing a short film?

Prepare as much as you can. When you have no money the time spent preparing is absolutely crucial. Never feel bashful about asking advice from others with more experience. The industry is very supportive in that way.

What advice do you have for directors trying to find a producer for a short film? Where's a good place to start?

Look at shorts programmes at your local art house cinema or a festival (*Brief Encounters*, *Halloween*, London and Edinburgh, for example) and see what takes you. It's always best to approach a producer whose work you identify with.

What do you enjoy most about producing short films?

The enjoyment of working with a team of people who are all doing it for the same reason, to make something you believe in and with the knowledge that if it goes well that it will lead to other collaborations.

INTERVIEW WITH WENDY BEVAN-MOGG (PRODUCER)

Wendy Bevan-Mogg is an accomplished film producer and screenwriter. She has produced numerous short films, music videos and feature-length productions and has recently formed the production company KUBISTA. She wrote and produced *Rare Books and Manuscripts*, which features on the accompanying DVD.

How did you get involved in producing short films?

I was working as a freelance script editor when I decided that I'd really like to produce my own piece. When I found the short story of *Rare Books* I just knew this was the film I wanted to make, so I just got on with it from there.

Roughly how many shorts have you produced?

Four or six, depending whether you count the *Straight 8s*.

Rare Books and Manuscripts

Evol

Dog Flap

The Space Between Us

Stiffy (Straight 8)

Space Man 8 (Straight 8)

I have also produced a music video.

What does your role as producer generally entail on a short film?

On short films, as with any project, my role as producer is to make sure the director has everything in place that he or she needs to make their film. I will either raise the finance or deal with any financial bodies involved in the film; then I'm location manager, production manager, line producer, post-production manager... you name it. Also, on my shorts I tend to have a strong creative input. Because of my background as a script editor, I work closely with the writer/director to ensure that the script is right before the film goes into pre-production.

Do you always use the same methods in producing them, or do different projects require different approaches?

Each film is different. More to the point each director is different – some are very hands off in pre-production, leaving much more to me, some prefer to work more independently. The different funding bodies also all require different levels of input, so you do find yourself having to satisfy lots of diverse requirements. However, the goals I have for each film are the same: to make sure that the script is right, that we shoot on the right format in the best possible locations, that the director is supported so that they make the film they want to make, and that the production values are as high as possible given the limits of the budget.

How has your experience of working in the film industry influenced your approach to producing short films?

Before I worked in shorts I was a script editor but also worked in sales and distribution. I therefore had a good working knowledge of the legal side of film-making (especially rights issues), which has been invaluable. I also spent years watching short films and going to festivals to see what the competition was like, what makes a good short film and how audiences respond to them.

Do you think that the more experience you have, the better you get at producing?

Definitely. Although I'm sure that if I knew then what I know now, I might not have started with *Rare Books*, which has been my biggest and most complicated production to date! *Rare Books* was effectively film school for me, though I'm constantly learning new things with every film I make.

What kind of skills do you need to be a good producer?

You need endless patience. Your job is very difficult, both practically and politically – you have to keep your director happy, allow him or her the space and resources to do their job, while at the same time you've got to stay on budget, within the law, find and look after the cast and crew, deal with any outside funding bodies, deliver on schedule, get the film out to festivals and all the while make it appear to the outside world that you're not stressed and always have time to answer questions or deal with the director's late night panics.

You might also find yourself guiding a new director through the entire process, it being film school for them too, which can be frustrating.

Then, you must also understand from the start that no matter how far you are instrumental in getting a film off the ground, the director will always get all the credit. This can take some getting used to, especially when festival guides often only quote the director's name next to the film title. Good directors do recognise their producer's input, but a producer must be aware that while one good short can start a director's career, a producer must have a slate of good films behind them.

What inspired you to write a screen adaptation of *Rare Books and Manuscripts*?

I knew from the moment I read the short story that it was perfect material for a short film. It had a clearly defined beginning, middle, twist and resolution, all within a short space of time. I also knew that it could be adapted to be almost silent (great for international festivals), and that the feel-good tone would go down very well with audiences. As far as actually writing the script was concerned, I just knew that I wanted to do it and that I'd at least have a go first – though I was prepared to admit defeat if necessary and find another writer. Luckily I didn't need to (and on the strength of this script I now have a writing agent and I'm now writing feature-length projects).

Did you have to get official rights to do an adaptation of Toby Litt's story, or did you just ask for permission?

Yes. I approached Toby's agent and purchased a short option on the story, just as you would when optioning a feature film. I then sent them both the script when it was done, and luckily they loved it and loved the film. Toby introduced it at the Port Eliot Literary Festival this year, and we hope to do more work together in the future.

Was it a long process, writing and developing the script?

It took about three months.

Did you work closely with Bruce Webb on the pre-production, on decisions such as choosing Mel Byers as DP etc, or were they mainly your decisions?

Bruce had worked with Mel before and brought her in as DP. She did a fantastic job, and I have been lucky enough to work with her again since.

Whose decision was it to shoot on 35mm? Did you look at other formats?

We originally planned to shoot on HD, but our investor allowed us to re-budget for 35mm.

How did you find Neve McIntosh? What was it that made you know she was right for the part?

Finding Neve was very serendipitous. Bruce, Elisabeth and I were all looking for actresses, and we all came up with Neve independently of each other! We did screen test her, but it was obvious as soon as we met her that she was perfect for the part. She is wonderful to work with and we all hope to work with her again. Casting Ian Mosby was great fun – Elisabeth and I went to Storm Models and asked to see a group of gorgeous blond men. That was a tough morning...!

Roughly how long did the pre-production take?

Three months.

Was it difficult finding and obtaining permission to use such good locations?

It wasn't too hard as we were filming in a university during the holidays. We are, however, hugely grateful to the UCL who, crucially, gave us a fantastic deal, without which we couldn't have shot there. Their staff were also really good to us, very flexible and understanding.

Where did you source your crew for the shoot?

We used a mixture of people we'd worked with before, recommendations from friends and also Shooting People. We were incredibly lucky with our crew; they were all superb and worked together fantastically well. I'm incredibly grateful to them for their hard work and professionalism. I have kept in contact with most of the crew and have used many of them on other shoots and will continue to do so.

How long did the shoot take? Did you encounter any major problems?

It was a four-day shoot. The camera broke down on day one, which was extremely stressful, and we had problems with the fire alarm, which went off four times! Apart from that we had no real problems (though it was a bit crowded when we were all squeezed into the flat for interior shots).

What kind of post-production workflow did you follow for the film, how far in advance had it been planned?

We arranged our post-production HODs before the shoot, but we didn't have a tight deadline so we took things as they came. We applied for and were awarded the UKFC Completion Funding for the film, which slowed us down a bit but gave us a sensible post-production budget, as well as a premiere in Edinburgh.

Roughly how long did post-production take?

It took approximately nine months, but this was largely because of stopping and waiting between November and March for the Film Council funding.

As the screenwriter did you find you were more involved creatively than you have been on other projects you have produced?

I was very involved, but this was largely in terms of casting, music etc rather than on the script. Bruce didn't change the script much, but when he did I knew that, with my producer's hat on, I had to accept this and not be too precious. It's a difficult balance, being writer/producer – I probably won't do it again on future projects, because you are so close to the material.

Did you find that the finished film was close to how you had imagined it when you were writing the script?

Very, very close. Better in some ways than I could have imagined, and different in others; but that's the nature of filmmaking. You never know what other people will bring to the project. I could never have imagined, for example, how wonderful Richard Lannoy's score would be. I'm very proud of the film.

What did you do with the film once it was completed? Did you have a distribution plan in mind beforehand?

The film premiered in Edinburgh, and has been going round the world since in festivals. It's been sold to TV in the UK and abroad. We signed the film to sales agency Dazzle before it was completed, which is unusual. The film's a year old now but we're still doing festivals and making sales.

What did you learn from making *Rare Books and Manuscripts*? In retrospect are there any things that you might have done differently?

I learnt everything from *Rare Books* – it was film school for me. There are things I would do differently now, but at the time it was just one great big learning curve.

What have you done since making *Rare Books and Manuscripts*?

Since making *Rare Books* I've made five other short films and a music video. I've also written a feature film, and I have a feature in development as producer.

What are your plans for the future?

I would like to continue writing and producing, and move on from shorts to features.

What advice would you give to people considering producing a short film?

Mainly to be realistic about the amount of time involved and also to be very clear about what you want to get out of it. To watch as many short films as you can to start with and, no matter what, to make sure that your script is the best it can possibly be before your shoot. As a final note too, not to be afraid of asking for the best stock, the best crew and the best cast you can get. There's no point in not aiming high just because it's 'only a short'.

What do you enjoy most about producing short films?

I enjoy the teamwork. But most of all I enjoy seeing the films on the big screen, remembering the journey and thinking, 'we did that'.

Figure 12. Still from *Rare Books and Manuscripts*. Produced by Wendy Bevan-Mogg.

6. PRE-PRODUCTION

Once you have completed a rough draft of a script, treatment or storyboard you are ready to begin pre-production. Pre-production is a process of preparation through which you calculate what you need to shoot your film and begin to organise and schedule for the shoot. Pre-production is also a period in which you hone your ideas and script.

Even though some short film ideas can be comparatively quick and easy to execute, breaking down and scheduling your idea will provide you with the most efficient way to get it made as well as provide you with experience for more complex future projects.

The essence of pre-production is organisation and planning. To many it's the least interesting phase of making a film, but the more time you spend on it – the more thorough you are – the better your shoot is going to go.

BREAKDOWNS

Once a rough copy of the script and/or storyboard has been completed, the director and producer can begin to break it down. The reason you break a script down is to produce a schedule that accounts for every detail of the script or storyboard, and therefore everything you need to make your film. Breakdowns and schedules allow you to find the most logical and practical way to shoot your film.

Breaking down a script entails combing through the script/storyboard and noting the technical and logistical requirements of each shot and each scene. Every element that will be required to create a scene needs to be noted down and should include all categories that appear on the breakdown sheet (see Figure 13).

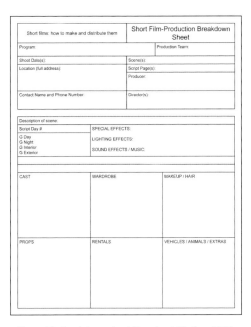

Figure 13. Breakdown sheet (downloadable from DVD).

Once all these requirements have been ascertained, it's then possible to evaluate them against the two key factors.

- Time
- Budget

This must be done scene by scene (rather than for the overall film) so that each can be evaluated for time and budget. Different types of scenes will have different values when it comes to the length of shooting time and the cost. This information and the importance of an individual scene can then be weighed up within the context of the whole film.

This process allows you to deal with the practicalities of the script. For example, a scene that takes place in a park at night might require a great deal of lighting and power. Securing access to the park location may also be complicated. Such factors may indicate that this scene is simply not practical within the time and budget limitations of the production. This scene must then be evaluated for its importance: is the dramatic information in that scene vital to the rest of the film? If not, perhaps it should simply be scratched. But if the scene is key to the rest of the film, then it needs to be reworked. Setting the action in the daytime could work, or changing the location to one that would be well-lit at night. If neither is an option, then you have to find another way to portray the dramatic information of that scene.

Breakdown sheets

The easiest way to collate all this information is to create breakdown sheets or use the ones provided with this book. Breakdown sheets should be duplicated and marked for each individual scene. Each one lists all the potential requirements a scene might necessitate, as well as the context, such as day or night time, interior or exterior. It is also important to note the scene number and page numbers, as well as give a very brief description of the key event in that scene.

Lining the script or storyboard

Lining the script should be done as you go through it to create the breakdown sheets. Using coloured markers that correlate with the colours on the breakdown sheets, you underline any occurrences in the script of cast, props etc that you need to mark on the breakdown sheets.

Production strips

Once you have completed the process of lining and breaking down the script or storyboard, you can compile much of the information into production strips.

Production strips are literally strips of card that you place on a strip board. They should be about 1cm wide and about 35cm long so that you can fit about ten to fifteen on the strip board. Conventionally, strip boards should allow you to slot the strips in and out so that they can be moved around easily but won't be easily displaced. If you are going to make your own, then you can use double-sided tape.

Each strip represents a scene or sequence within your script and should contain the information from the breakdown sheets; especially important is the scene number, page number and scene description.

You will now also need to give each of the characters in your script a number that will be used on the board to refer to that character.

This information is compiled on the strip in the order that it lines up with the header on the strip board. You should start with the header information first and then work down through the categories.

You can also use colour-coded strips to present information. For instance, you could select colours for interior and exterior scenes, for day and night, or for individual locations. The colours you choose are entirely up to you; this is done purely to help you and others see the information more easily.

This may seem like a long-winded process, but what you have done is broken down your entire film and its needs into units, which can simply and quickly be configured into combinations that will allow you to create the most practical schedule for your film as well as provide budget breakdowns.

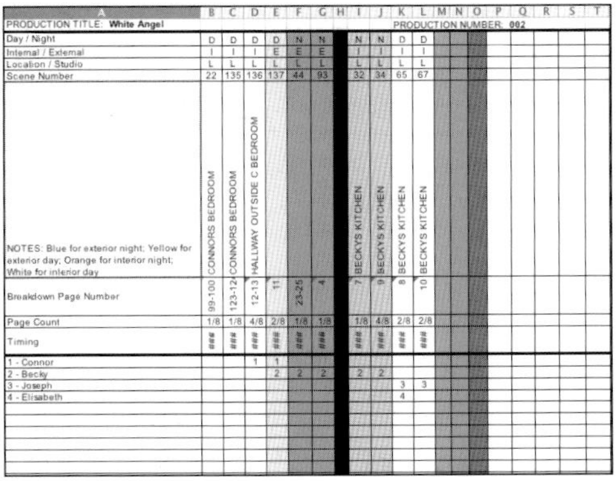

Figure 14.
Example of a software strip board.

SOFTWARE SCHEDULING

If you don't fancy getting out your crayons, scissors and ruler, then the alternative option is to use scheduling software. Software programmes work on exactly the same principle but allow you to fill in and shift around information on screen. Breakdown sheets, strip boards, shot lists, schedules and budgets can all be collated in one programme that allows you to print off the definitive versions. There are many downloadable programmes online that all essentially perform the same task and range in price from £20 to £350, the cheapest being filmmakers software. TM/http://www.filmmakersoftware.com

SCHEDULING

Once you have created your production strips you will instantly be able to see the major common factors between them, such as the location or actors required in each scene. Based on this, you can begin to place your strips into an order, so strips with the most important common factors can go next to each other, all the shots at one location next, or all the exterior night time shots. You will quickly realise that this is creating a very different running order to that of your script, but a much more practical one in which to shoot.

The two main factors that should govern your arrangement of the strips are the actors and the locations. You want to use your cast as efficiently as possible, so you want to avoid having an actor turn up every day for a week to deliver one line of dialogue even if that is how it might appear in the script. Ideally you want to shoot all their action on one day. You need to work with the same efficiency when it comes to locations, especially if you are hiring them.

You will also need to work out how much you can shoot in a day. Unfortunately there is no such thing as a ratio of how long a page of script takes to film. This will depend on the nature of the production, the cast, the crew and the complexity of the scene, as well as an infinite amount of unquantifiable factors.

When trying to estimate how much to shoot in a day, the best policy is to imagine how much time you think it will take, and then double it. There is no point trying to pack as much as is humanly possible into the time; if you then don't achieve this for any reason, the rest of your schedule will be useless. If you have never made a film before, then be especially careful to over estimate how much time you need.

The experience of your crew and cast will have a huge impact on your daily quotas, as well as access to locations. If you are shooting exteriors, then the weather and time of year will also dictate how much you can achieve.

With short filmmaking things will always take much longer than you anticipate, with plenty of unforeseen, random setbacks. Realistically accounting for the variables, set up and turnaround times should give you a schedule that will be able to accommodate most eventualities.

SCHEDULE DATES

Once you have a schedule that provides the shooting order of your film, you then need to find the actual date that you can begin. Due to short film's low-budget nature, this is often a difficult aspect of scheduling. Ideally one might start on a given date and then shoot the film every day until it is finished, but this is often impossible. Due to the costs of hiring equipment and a cast and crew that may be working in kind, short filmmakers have to be extremely flexible when it comes to fixing dates. Weekends are generally the optimum time, as crew and cast are less likely to be working on other projects and equipment can often be hired on a Friday and returned on a Monday, providing a three-day period for a single day's rental.

When scheduling a film on a floating basis, based around the availability of cast and crew as well as locations and equipment, it is often a good idea to have a deadline in place. Whether this is a film festival that you want to send your film to, or a self-organised premiere, deadlines will help keep the production motivated, with a fixed goal in mind.

CALL SHEETS

Once the overall shooting schedule has been locked and dates set, call sheets can then be drawn up. Call sheets give a detailed breakdown of the times, events and scenes that will be covered for a single day of the schedule.

For a shoot of only a few days, it is possible to draw up just one call sheet for the entire shoot. But generally they are handed out at the end of the day's shoot, so that any amendments, such as shots that didn't get shot, can be transferred to the next day. The call sheet provides information for both the cast and crew, giving individual times for the actors to arrive, be in make up and then costume, before being on set for their scenes. It also provides crew with pick-up times, break times and indications of how much time has been allotted for various set ups and strikes. Similar to the overall schedule, it is important to be realistic about the time you allow for the eventualities of a call sheet, allowing enough time for people to perform their jobs properly, but not leaving people hanging around waiting for other departments. (A call sheet template can be downloaded from the accompanying DVD.)

SHOT LIST

Some short films are often easy to schedule, potentially only requiring a day of shooting in one location with minimal cast and crew; others may require shooting for a whole week or multiple weekends over several months. Each of these scenarios will require very different types of schedule, but there is a common factor: each of the shooting days needs to be broken down not only into the order in which to shoot the scenes, but also the order of the individual shots that make up those scenes.

Just like creating the daily schedule for the production, a shot list works on a similar principle: all the shots that make up the entire film need to be listed so that an order in which to shoot them can be organised. Again the aim is to produce a list of shots that gives you the most practical and efficient order in which to shoot the film.

On a storyboard you will have all the shots in the sequence that you want the finished film to occur. The first step is to number each of the shots on the storyboard in that order. Then analyse each shot and work out the shooting order. For instance, a scene involving a conversation between two people will potentially involve two different camera positions (set ups) – let's call them position A and B – from which you will use different lenses to shoot wide, medium and close up shots. In your storyboard, the sequence of shots would run 1,2,3,4,5 etc but this might involve cutting between a wide shot from position A to a medium shot from position B, then back to A for another wide and then B for a close up, potentially shifting between different shots from A and B positions many times within a scene. Obviously to film the scene in the storyboard order would entail moving the camera every time there was a change of position, which would be both laborious and time-consuming. So instead, all the shots from a camera position A need to be shot in a block before moving on to position B. However, a shot list isn't just a list of camera positions, the individual shots themselves need to be listed. So again you would go through the storyboard and note all the shots from position A that were wide, medium and close ups and then put those in order, perhaps starting with all the wide shots first and then moving through the rest until all the types of shot from position A have been listed; then move on to the next set up of position B and start again. This would result in a shot list that might run out of sequence, for instance 2,5,6,9,13.

The next step is to give a description of the type of shot, potentially using abbreviations. Wide shot (WS), close up (CU) etc and a brief description of the action taking place in that frame of the storyboard. So as a simple example:

SET UP A

Shot 1 A (WS) Woman sits alone at restaurant table

Shot 12 A (WS) Woman leaves envelope on table and sips drink

Shot 3 A (MS) Woman looks man up and down

Shot 7 A (MS) Woman looks down at envelope

Shot 9 A (CU) Woman nods at man

Shot 8 A (CU) Woman picks up envelope to feel the weight

SET UP B

Shot 11 B (WS) Man gets up and leaves

Shot 2 B (WS) Man enters restaurant and sits opposite her

Shot 5 B (MS) Man reaches into coat and pulls out envelope

Shot 4 B (CU) Man stares back

Shot 10 B (CU) Man nods at woman

Shot 6 B (CU) Man slides envelope across table

In the storyboard, and potentially the finished film, however, the shots would run like this.

Shot 1 A (WS) Woman sits alone at restaurant table

Shot 2 B (WS) Man enters restaurant and sits opposite her

Shot 3 A (MS) Woman looks man up and down

Shot 4 B (CU) Man stares back

Shot 5 B (MS) Man reaches into coat and pulls out envelope

Shot 6 B (CU) Man slides envelope across table

Shot 7 A (MS) Woman looks down at envelope

Shot 8 A (CU) Woman picks up envelope to feel the weight

Shot 9 A (CU) Woman nods at man

Shot 10 B (CU) Man nods at woman

Shot 11 B (WS) Man gets up and leaves

Shot 12 A (WS) Woman leaves envelope on table and sips drink

SHOT LIST TIPS

As you will have noticed from this simple example, a complex range of shots can be obtained from just two camera set ups, by using different lenses or a zoom set at different focal lengths. This then provides plenty of coverage to create a dynamically edited scene. Looking at the shot list it would potentially be possible to shoot the establishing wide shot of the woman as a master scene shot (see directing), shooting an entire run-through of the scene from that set up and type of shot, so that shots 1 and 12 were the beginning and end of one take, providing continuity in case there were any gaps in the remaining coverage. The other key point that can emerge when compiling a shot list is how crucial the camera positioning is. Limiting the amount of set ups will save crucial time when shooting various shots; minimal but well-chosen camera positions should create a scenario that makes use of lenses to move the perspective of the camera, rather than having to move the camera over and over again. Floor plans can also be hugely beneficial when combined with a storyboard and shot list. Using basic layouts of the sets or locations, it is possible to mark out where the camera would ideally be placed, giving the different set ups numbers or letters and allowing the crew to reference where the camera is going.

BUDGET

Once you have completed your breakdowns and schedule, you can start to see all the elements that your film requires to be made. Whether this is time, locations, equipment, cast, crew or probably a combination of them all, you are now ready to work out how much it will all cost.

Although 'no budget' is an ubiquitous term within filmmaking, the unfortunate truth is that there is no such thing as a film made without a budget. 'No budget' really means 'no film', and is a term used to compare multi-million-pound feature film budgets with short film or indie feature film budgets, that are comparatively so minute they might be perceived as non-existent.

Any filmmaking, short or otherwise, is potentially extremely expensive. It may cost the same as the hairdressing budget of a Hollywood blockbuster, but that can be tens of thousands of pounds. However, it is possible to make a short film for very, very little. Borrowing equipment and only paying for tape stock means it is possible to create a perfectly executed short for under £20, it just depends on the resources available to you and the production values you want the film to have.

Whether the budget of your film requires only £100 or £10,000, it's important that you are actually sure it can be produced for that amount. To decide this, you need to create a thorough budget, listing everything that you need and how much each item will cost.

LINE BUDGETS

Conventionally, film budgets are broken down into two types of category, above the line and below the line. Above the line costs are flat fees for the entire run of the film; conventionally, this includes directors' and actors' salaries as well as script rights and any other flat payments. Below the line costs include everything else: location hire, equipment hire, stock, editing time, crew hire etc.

This type of line budget is not always necessary for short filmmakers, however; often script rights, proc   id director fees are non-existent and the things that really nee   th b   geted for are equipment and stock.

SHORT FILM BUDGE

With short films it's often easier to simply break your budget into three simple sections. This allows you to keep the budget organised and see more clearly at which stages you will need certain sums of money.

- Pre-Production
- Production
- Post-Production

TOP SHEET

Film budgets of any size normally follow the same principle. Rather than consisting of a list of all the individual costs involved that could go on for pages, the costs are broken down into larger categories. These categories are listed

9	SOUND & MUSIC				
	COMPOSER			150	150
	STOCK MUSIC / SOUND EFFECTS			68	68
	STUDIO HIRE			1600	1600
	TRANSFERS			575	575
	MIXING			80	80
10	EDITING AND FINISHING				
	EDITOR			0	0
	SOUND EDITOR			0	0
	EDITING TIME			275	275
	TITLES CREDITS			0	0
	EFFECTS			0	0
	GRADING			0	0
	TRANSFER			430	430
	STOCK			750	750
	PRINTS			0	0
11	DISTRIBUTION				
	PREVIEW COPIES			325	325
	PUBLICITY			250	250
	CINEMA HIRE			160	160
	PRESS KIT			230	230
	STILLS			80	80
	FESTIVAL SUBMISSION FEES			325	325
12	CONTINGENCY				
	PERCENTAGE			750	750
	Total			8456	8456

Figure 15.
Budget top sheet.

on the top sheet of the budget, with the category costs added together to provide a grand total. These categories then have separate pages, where the individual costs that make them up are listed.

The top sheet serves two functions: it both gives an instant indication of how your film budget is balanced, and provides the page numbers where the categories can be found, allowing the individual items to be found or amended quickly.

Contingency

The important thing to bear in mind when putting a budget together is that budgets in filmmaking rarely come in less than planned. Generally films have a tendency to go over budget. Not necessarily because items have been omitted from the budget, but simply because it is difficult to remain within budget when so many variables are involved. For this reason, it's common practice to add a contingency or miscellaneous category – generally 10% of the overall budget – which is there to cover any unforeseen events or costs that occur.

7. PRODUCTION VALUES

Production values is an expression that is used to refer to the finished look of the film, and comes from the methods and tools used to make it. In general filmmakers aim for the highest production values they can achieve on their budget. Although some films may intentionally opt for a lo-tech look because it reflects the subject matter or themes they are working with.

You will probably be familiar with feature films, music promos and commercials that have a variety of distinct or subtle visual styles that are often distinguishable from each other. All of these styles are achieved by a series of creative decisions taken over format, set design, lighting and costume; all of these contribute to the look and feel of the finished film.

Although generally governed by the film's budget, high production values don't necessarily have to involve huge sums of money. Spending time rather than budget on as many different visual aspects as you can, whether it's wardrobe, art department or grading and title sequences, you can still produce a great-looking film for very little.

FUNDING

In most countries there are a variety of funding organisations and film commissioning bodies that offer funding schemes for short filmmakers to realise entire projects, complete them or fund film prints for distribution (see resources).

Private funding is often the only way that short filmmakers have to fund their films, however. Many films are entirely funded by the director and producer. Due to short films' non-commercial nature, financially backing short films is not an investment that will guarantee returns, which often makes it difficult to find investors. Professional producers are occasionally able to find individuals or production companies willing to back short films, but this is fairly rare. The most common type of private funding for short films tends to be in-kind crew services either from crew or rental or post houses offering support through discounts.

TYPES OF FUNDING

Match funding

Match funding is the funding of a partial amount of the entire filmmaking budget. This is common in filmmaking where, due to the high costs involved, various funding bodies will offer specific amounts to make up the whole budget.

Completion funding

Completion funding is a common occurrence in short filmmaking and provides funding to films at the rough cut stage in order that post-production can be completed. Films often run over and out of budget for the final post-production stages, which can be the most expensive, but at this point, with a nearly complete version of the film, it is often possible to gain support for the project.

APPLYING FOR FUNDING

For anyone, whether an individual or funding body, to offer financial backing to a short film project, they will need to consider it worthwhile on a creative level, but also be convinced that the people involved are experienced enough to bring it to fruition.

The key here is professionalism. Presenting a well-structured and thought-out production will be essential to securing funding. Storyboards, budgets and distribution strategies will all need to be carefully put together and presented with the same production standards and attention to detail that you would like your finished film to have.

8. CASTING

Having honed your idea into a script, you need to find the actors to play the roles. However good your idea or script is, without the right actors to bring it to life then the strengths of the material won't be reflected in your final film.

Finding the right actors can be a long process, but one that can influence the final outcome of your film more than any other. Both your approach to directing, and the nature of your material, will dictate your approach to casting. You may have people in mind for the idea or script as you are developing it, in which case it could simply be a matter of finding the right time when they are available for your shoot. You may find that the actions of the characters are the focus of your film rather than their emotions, and decide that you can get away without professional actors.

If your film does require a cast you are more than likely going to need to go through a casting process to find the most suitable people.

CASTING PROFESSIONAL ACTORS

Casting actors with skill and experience is going to make a significant difference not only to your finished film but also to the ease with which you make it. You shouldn't underestimate just how significant the talents of an actor can be in bringing a role to life. Even roles that require little or no dialogue to be delivered, or little obvious display of emotion, will still benefit from an actor's ability with body language. A professional actor will not only bring their expertise to the project, but also their professionalism. This will have a two-fold effect on your film. The actor's ability should allow you to achieve the type of performance that you want much faster and in fewer takes. You should then be able to shoot your film faster and more efficiently while having more usable takes to edit with. All of this will of course depend on your successful direction, but selecting the right actor with enough ability for the demands of the role will strengthen that possibility.

CASTING NON-PROFESSIONAL ACTORS

When developing an idea or script for a short film, you may well be working from your own personal experience or the experiences of people that you know in which case it is inevitable that the characters involved will be directly or indirectly based on people that you know or have met. You may then want to ask them to take on the roles in your film. Straightforward as this may sound, using a friend or acquaintance to play either themself or a similar character can be complicated. They may have no problem behaving naturally in normal, day-to day situations, but could find it difficult to recreate this naturalness when acting out past events or fictional scenarios.

Because films are shot non-chronologically, scenes and individual lines of dialogue may need to be delivered back to back with others of often contrasting emotion. This can be demanding for talented professionals and may be just too much to expect from amateurs. The other major factor to consider when casting non-professionals is the stage fright factor. People may well be able to perform in front of an impromptu audience or in rehearsals, but once in front of the camera and lights, they can become overwhelmed by the pressure to perform. Of course you may be able to achieve outstanding results with amateur or novice actors, capturing a rawness that professionals would strive for, but you do need to be prepared for the time and patience this can take.

FINDING ACTORS

Luckily for filmmakers the number of actors in the world far outweighs the number of directors. There are enormous amounts of amateur and professional actors who are available for film work. The problem is finding the right ones for your film. It is often a good strategy to try as many avenues as you can find and search as widely as possible, before beginning to narrow the selection down.

Advertising

Advertising for roles in your film can be an effective method of finding actors. There are several different domains where you can advertise, all of which can be worthwhile. You or your producer will need to put an ad together giving the details of the film and the specifics of the roles. Try and make it seem both as interesting and worthwhile as you can, and there shouldn't be any need to exaggerate the scale or style of production.

When placing an ad, you should provide the following information:

- Synopsis of the film
- Breakdown of the parts available
- Description of the characteristics of the parts
- Description of any special requirements for the role (nudity etc)
- Approximate estimation of how long the shoot will take
- Approximate estimation of when it will take place
- Specify where the shoot will take place
- State whether it is paid work
- State whether the film is self-funded or who it is funded by
- What you require for application for the role (CV, head shots etc)
- Contact information

Acting schools

Acting schools are some of the best places to place ads. You will often get a positive response from students and find a range of talented and motivated individuals, looking to showcase their potential. Equally, visiting local theatre productions will potentially give you an opportunity to check out people's ability and find talent for your film.

Internet message forums

Internet message forums vary greatly. Many of them are designed for amateur actors and agents, as well as directors and producers. These sites are two dimensional, so that they provide databases for actors to post their CVs and head shots, and also allow productions to post advertisements looking for cast. This means that you can post an ad and also spend time trawling through the database for potential possibilities. Many sites offer filtering so that you can narrow down your search by gender, age group etc. Some sites require a joining or subscription fee, but this is often for posting your acting credentials, rather than posting an ad for work.

Internet databases

There are many professional Internet databases for professional actors. Some of them are directly related to actors' unions and are run for the theatre and film industries. Because of this many of them will have substantial joining fees or charge fees for contact information. This can be a worthwhile investment as the quality of the talent on these sites will be worth paying for (see www.spotlight.com and www.uk.castingcallpro.com).

Figure 16.
castingcallpro.com

Casting agents

Casting agents deal solely with casting actors for film, television or theatre. They can be extremely useful, often opening up possibilities that you might not otherwise be aware of. Casting agents will generally liaise with the producer and director to find out exactly what kind of actor or actress you want for the roles, and then use a combination of techniques to find the right actors.

Rather than simply undertake any advertising and co-ordination on your behalf, the casting agent will rely on an in-depth knowledge of actors and already be familiar with their talent and range. In addition to access to professional databases, this will allow them to narrow your search down very quickly. They will then organise castings for you to attend, and once you have narrowed down your search, negotiate with actors and agents over contracts and fees.

Narrowing down the selection

From applicants' résumé's and head shots, you should be able to create a shortlist of people that will be suitable for given roles. The casting director (if you have one) or you will then contact them with dates for a live casting.

Holding a casting

Depending how many roles and applicants you get, you need to decide on a venue, such as a rehearsal space, and methodically work out a schedule for arrival times so that you don't leave people waiting indefinitely. Castings can be as rigorous or easygoing as you want. You can potentially email actors the script and then hold read-throughs of specific scenes at the casting, or simply ask them to perform a set piece that they feel comfortable with. If you are new to directing this may well be your first opportunity to start practicing your own communication skills and develop a working method with actors.

Callbacks

It is common practice to record castings on video. Together with any notes you have made, this will allow you to spend time going over the options before making your final choices. Sometimes the decision process can take a long time and you may feel that you need to hold a callback for a couple of roles, either later the same day or on another occasion.

Hiring actors

If the actors you choose have an agent or agency, then all negotiation of fees will be done via them. If your actors don't, then you can work out fees directly. Even if your actors agree to work for free, due to budget constraints, you should still draw up a contract containing dates and times, as well as the terms of the agreement.

Release forms

Getting any cast members that appear in your film to sign release forms is mandatory. Whether a professional actor or not, they have to give written consent for the film to be publicly screened. Although this is often not an issue for screening at film festivals, any television broadcast will generally require copies of release forms signed by participating cast. (A release form template can be downloaded from the accompanying DVD.)

INTERVIEW WITH ROSALIE CLAYTON (CASTING AGENT)

Rosalie Clayton spent several years working for Nina Gold as a casting agent, before setting up her own casting agency. She has cast everything from theatre productions to feature films, and of course short films.

How did you become a casting director?

I first got into casting when I was working as an assistant director at a theatre. They had no casting system, they would see 30 people per role and as I already had a good knowledge of actors I just seemed to take over the casting process. Before I knew it I was no longer their assistant director I was their casting director. I really enjoyed casting and when a musical I cast called 'Pageant' transferred to the West End I decided to really go in that direction and worked for people in TV & film as a casting assistant before setting up my own company.

When a director or producer contacts you with a script, how do you proceed from there?

It is hard to put into words and I guess everyone has their own system but for me I read the script at least two times so that I can really make up a mental picture of the characters, their settings, etc. I suppose I put my own vision onto the script and characters completely – their mannerisms, their look, weight, everything, and then I talk with the producer and director to hear how they see the characters. If their vision is totally different I have to rethink the character completely. If their idea of the character is slightly different, I will bring in actors that both fit their idea and some who fit my vision. But many times I am able to bring in whoever I feel is right as long as they fit into the general age, etc. described and then through the audition process things may change.

How do you go about finding the right kind of actors for a role?

After years of going to the theatre three times a week I have a pretty good knowledge of actors out there so I will usually have a good list of who I would like to see for the role straight away. I also brief out to agents because they can really come up with some interesting ideas and remind me of people I haven't seen before. If the part is really hard to cast I will hold auditions by myself of actors that have been recommended before putting the good ones before the director and producer.

How does a casting normally unfold and how long do they take?

Sometimes a job you think will be a breeze will go on forever and sometimes what looks like the hardest job can be cast in a couple of sessions. It all depends on actors' availability and how people work.

Once the director has chosen actors for the various roles, what is the next step?

I call the agent, check they are available and if so I book them. Once money and dates have been agreed I send a casting advice note to the production company, which outlines the payment and special stipulations, so that they can send out a contract.

Is there a standard rate for actors?

Not any more. It depends on the nature of the project. But things have changed so much in the last few years re fees that you can never tell which actors will do what for what money. I think for short films it is always good to pay something if you can – even if it is only £50 per day it makes a big difference. Like all things, the more money you can pay the better but most actors know that short films are made on little money and are happy with expenses.

What about the hours you might expect them to be on set, is there a standard limit?

It depends. Ten-hour days is a good limit if people are doing you a favour.

Do you do the negotiation over fees with actors' agents or is this up to the producer?

I usually do the deals – it is easier most of the time because I will have a relationship with the agent and it is my job to know what the actor has done before and therefore what we are negotiating on.

Is there a standard contract as far as hiring actors for short films is concerned, and what kind of information is normally included?

Equity have a sample short film contract but as long as there is something in writing outlining the fee, usage, travel arrangement and accommodation if needed, it works.

What happens if an actor doesn't have an agent?

The same process happens but directly with the actor.

Do you ever go on set during a production and why?

Yes, if I have time, it is good to follow through on things and make sure everybody is okay and happy with each other.

What can the producer and director do to make your life easier?

It is a massive help when the producer and director know what they want. If they direct an actor in auditions to get what they want rather than expecting their vision just to walk through the door then it's a godsend for both myself and the actor. Actors are not mind readers and they need pointing in the right direction sometimes to play the role the way the director wants. The reason I will have brought them in is because I think they can do that but it may need a little work.

What advice do you have for directors and producers who are trying to cast for a short film?

Get help with casting if you can, put breakdowns in publications, audition actors to find the right person for the job, and if you feel the need to go with a 'name' aim high but be realistic. You can get some lovely actors to work on your project but it takes a while to put all that into place.

How would you go about finding a casting agent for a short film?

It never hurts to approach casting directors whose work you have seen and liked. If they don't want to cast your project they may have an assistant who would love to or they may recommend someone. Ask other producers who they have used.

9. WHERE TO SHOOT YOUR FILM

LOCATIONS

Finding the right locations to shoot your short film can be as straightforward as using your own home, or as complicated as hiring a whole street.

The first step in finding the locations you need for your film is to look at your script and your storyboard and work out the type of environment you think suits the story. Then begin scouting for those types of locations. The earlier you start this process the more likely you are to find what you are looking for. The perfect location, however simple, can make a huge difference to your finished film, reflecting the mood of the material and emphasising characters' actions.

SCOUTING

There are two ways to scout for locations, either through databases or out on foot. Which you choose will depend on the needs of the film and the budget you are working with.

Location databases

Location databases come in all shapes and sizes. Depending on the region you are planning to shoot in, there will probably be a range of location services including catalogues of potential film locations either at their offices or online. These are often run as businesses or will be a facility of the local film commission for that area. A location database that runs as a business will

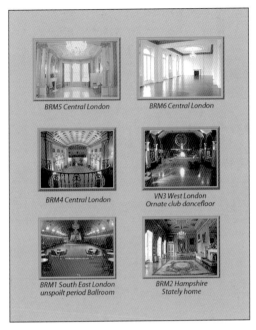

Figure 17. Online location database at www.locations-uk.com

often charge substantial fees for securing a location through their outfit. This is extra to the daily rate of hiring the location from the owners. This means that you might not have a chance to strike a deal with the location owners, as it will be brokered by the agency. Unless you are on a substantial budget, it is much more practical to do your own research.

Local film commissions can be very knowledgeable about locations you might be interested in. They will also have extensive databases of locations that have been used for filming and a good idea of how much they will cost to hire. Based on both the needs of your film and your budget, they should be able to point you in the right direction.

If you are shooting within your local area, then you may well be familiar with the locations you want to use. If you are shooting in another area then it's a good idea to ask advice from people who are familiar with it.

Local councils will have knowledge of places available for filming and can also put you in touch with the relevant departments. City councils will have their own film officer who will be able to advise you on protocol for securing a licence to shoot on council locations.

If you opt for privately owned buildings you can secure permission and negotiate fees with the owners, while public places or buildings will require you to contact the governing authority.

RECCE

However good a location may appear in a photo or sound from a description, it may well not suit the needs of your film. Every location in which you want to shoot needs to be visited by at least yourself and your DP. Before you get to the stage of securing permission or paying a hire fee, you will need to evaluate whether it is possible to shoot the desired scenes there. Many locations may be aesthetically perfect for your film, but implausible on a practical level. These are the factors that you should consider when you recce potential locations:

Light

Does the location have enough available light to film in, taking into account the time of day you will want to shoot there as well as the dates?

If not, is it possible to light it artificially, bearing in mind that large locations need large amounts of lighting to light them? This is a crucial factor that your DP will have to consider.

Sound

What are the acoustics like? Is there background noise? Will there be any other noise at the time you want to shoot? Locations with bad acoustics can make sound recording difficult or impossible. Your sound recordist should be consulted and potentially recce any locations that you are unsure about.

Traffic

Busy public places are an extremely difficult place to shoot in. The variables that can occur while shooting multiply as soon as you add a crowd, traffic or busy street to the scenario, and quiet areas can easily have their own rush hour periods.

Power

You can run a camera from a battery, but any serious lighting is going to require a dedicated power supply. If you're shooting exteriors, you need to see if you can draw power from anywhere indoors, or run from a generator. If you're shooting interiors then the same applies (see lighting).

Space

Is there really enough to get your crew and cast in the same location along with your gear? You will need to set up some kind of unit base and access to conveniences etc. Is there parking for your cast and crew? Does this need to be arranged? Is it possible to get your equipment to the location if not? Remember that cramped working environments make a difficult job harder.

Short of using your own place or borrowing a location from a friend, most private locations, whether you have hired them for a fee or not, will need you to provide accurate information about the nature of your film as well as provide proof of insurance for the location.

Licences

Filming in public locations requires you by law to liaise with the local authority and the local police department. Many local types of council will require you to apply for a licence that will then permit you to film in a specific area.

Short films with a small crew of less than ten will often be able to get a special licence that is less stringent than that required for a bigger production. However, you will still have to obey the same health and safety guide-lines and provide proof of insurance.

Location manager

Location managers deal with sourcing and negotiating locations. Anything that concerns a location is their domain. Most short film productions don't have one, but if your short requires lots of locations and you can delegate this responsibility to someone else, then it will help with production.

STUDIOS

If you need to create an extremely controlled environment, or build a set of considerable scale for your film, then you are going to need to hire a studio or soundstage.

Shooting in a studio environment offers you nearly endless potential as a filmmaker. It is possible with enough time and resources to create just about any scenic or lighting arrangement that you could need. This is what makes shooting in studios so desirable; unlike locations you can create con-ditions where lighting and sound can be kept constant, circumstances that you would not otherwise be able to achieve.

On location you will often be working around factors such as background noise and bad acoustics, constantly fluctuating light or not enough, and the general upheaval of everyday life that can make filming slow or just com-pletely impossible.

In a studio you can create bespoke sets that will be designed for the needs of your film: rooms without ceilings, views with permanent sunsets or differ-ent planets altogether. All of which can be maintained for days on end until you have finished shooting.

The drawback to this freedom is that shooting in a studio is expensive. A day rate for even a small soundstage professionally equipped for filming can be many times more expensive than the entire budget of many short films. This alone puts shooting your short in the confines of a professional studio beyond the means of most short filmmakers. It is, however, possible to find spaces where you can potentially set up your own studio (see non-professional studios).

If your film requires a studio set up and the budget is sizable enough to hire one, then these are the factors you need to consider:

NON-PROFESSIONAL STUDIOS

It is possible to find places that can be used as a film studio, or even photographic studios that will allow you to film. Sports halls, warehouses and large photographic studios are all often sizable enough to shoot a short film in. These places will often be hireable for a fraction of the price that professional film studios will cost. The drawback to this logic is that these places are not equipped for the needs of shooting a film and often by the time you have equipped them you may well have spent as much as it would have cost you to shoot at a professional premises. These are the factors you should carefully consider and budget before you make a decision.

These types of buildings will not be soundproofed, so you could potentially have background noise issues. Due to the size and shape of these buildings the acoustics will more often than not be terrible The only way to tackle this would be to soundproof the building, which would be an impossibility.

There will be no grid from which to suspend lights from the ceiling, or backdrops or drapes. You would need to hire scaffolding and at least one rigger to put it up to achieve anything close to what you would have in a studio. It would take at least a day each for both set up and strike (i.e. the dismantling of a set for a scene, which only takes place when it is definitely not going to be needed for other shots).

The power supplies for these places will not be capable of supplying the amount of electricity you will need to light a space of that size. This means that you would need to hire petrol-driven generators that will need to be outside the building and run cables inside for your lighting. Obviously you will also need some petrol.

You may also have great difficulty getting insurers to insure you for making a film in such places, simply because they are not designed for filmmaking and so the health and safety issues are exacerbated. You may well need to have a security guard.

All these factors add up financially and practically and it can be an organisational nightmare for what often ends up being a small saving. In a professional studio you will generally have everything in one place. It will be a short walk or shorter run to find just about anything you could possibly need in the middle of a shoot.

SOUNDSTAGES

Soundstages come in all shapes and sizes, ranging from the size of a tennis court to the size of a football pitch, with price tags to match. They are designed and maintained for filmmaking, but are essentially empty spaces, which means you will need to create or hire in everything that your film requires.

They are called soundstages because they are completely soundproofed. Once the doors are shut then you have perfect acoustics for sound recording that will remain uninterrupted until you open the doors again. Some studios will have stages that are not soundproofed, which will often be considerably cheaper than soundstages and ideal for shooting films with no dialogue or live sound recording.

As with most filmmaking equipment, hire prices will be quoted by the day or for a four-day week. Prices are often negotiable, but don't expect to be able to compete with feature films or commercials for space or time. Studios often have what is known as down time, where soundstages are dormant – i.e. not in use – and this can sometimes be for very extended periods. The best strategy for obtaining a studio soundstage at a discounted rate is often to find out when these periods might occur, so that you are working around their schedule rather than them working around yours.

Grid

Soundstages have very high ceilings, designed to accommodate large amounts of lighting, while still leaving plenty of headroom for filming. The ceilings of soundstages are equipped with a grid made from intersecting girders that span the length and width of the stage. Lighting plans can be designed in advance of the shoot and then conformed to this structure by the gaffers and sparks.

Cyclorama/cove

Soundstages will often have a cyclorama (cyc). Constructed from canvas, wood or both, the cove goes from floor to ceiling and seamlessly curves round the contours of the studio walls.

The cyc can be used for paintings of large scenic backdrops or as a uniform shade of green, for chroma key effects for example. Many studios have a policy that the cove is left as is, from the last shoot that took place there. This is an important consideration and if you are planning to use the cove as a backdrop you will need to budget for an adequate amount of paint to cover the walls and floor, as well as the time and facilities to change it to whatever

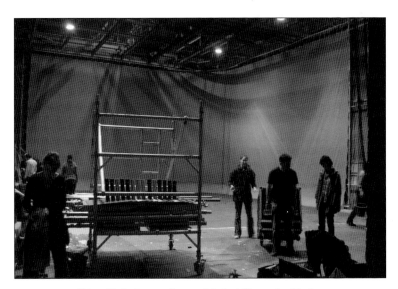

Figure 18. Cyclorama of a soundstage at Shepperton Studios.

colour or scene you require. This will probably involve hiring a tower to cover the dimensions completely. Many studios will have on-site painters who can re-spray a cove in a matter of hours and will quote with or without supplying the paint.

Lighting/power

Soundstages can be huge. To light an environment of such a scale can take a great deal of lighting. As attractive as the possibilities of shooting in a huge studio might be, if you can't afford the amount of lighting that you need for the space then the potential to make proper use of it isn't really there. Even ambient lighting for a small soundstage can require several trucks full of lights and cables.

Professional gaffers and sparks are essential for setting up this quantity of lighting and will need to be on hand throughout the shoot, even for minor changes that may need making. Contractually, the studio is unlikely to let non-professional gaffers or sparks operate in their spaces and it would be dangerous for untrained members of the crew to attempt to do so.

Soundstages are equipped with three-phase power supplies. Domestic single-phase power supplies might be able to handle a few small film lights but cannot deliver anywhere near the amounts needed for studio-style set ups. Three-phase power is a transmission system designed for supplying constant amounts of power to large loads such as film lighting. Another important budgetary consideration to bear in mind is that the studio will charge you for the amount of electricity you use while hiring the stage. Although this is dependent on how long and how much lighting you are using the amounts can often be very substantial and should not be overlooked.

Services

Larger studio complexes are often like small towns, not necessarily in size but because they provide a full set of filmmaking services. Independent companies will normally be based at larger film studios so it is often possible to find most things you will need to hire or buy within the studio itself. This is not always the case, however, so it is worthwhile checking just what services are available when making your decision about which studio to choose.

Having everything based at the one location is ideal. You will potentially be able to hire your entire equipment for the film from that one spot. Camera equipment, lighting, props and costumes, special effects along with timber merchants, scaffolding and drape hire companies. The time it would normally take to collect or have all these things delivered can thus be minimised, making the coordination of the production considerably simpler, and often saving significantly on transport costs.

Equally, if something goes wrong, breaks down or is overlooked in the hire, you won't have to stop shooting for long before it can be obtained.

Film studios will often have other facilities ranging from video conferencing to screening rooms, but what should interest you most are changing rooms, hair and make up rooms, and catering.

Along with your soundstage you may well need to book additional rooms. You generally won't want, or indeed be able, to have hair and make up or costume changes taking place on set, so specific rooms located in close proximity to the soundstage are equipped for this.

Catering is also a major consideration. Studios will often have canteens and restaurants on site; either you can buy vouchers to hand out to your cast and crew or they can sign for their food and you pick up the bill at the end of the shoot. This is also much more convenient then having to organise independent catering.

Health and safety

Film studios will have extremely stringent health and safety rules. You or your producer will need to sign declarations to say that their guidelines will be followed. Lists of all members of the cast and crew will have to be provided and all crew involved in rigging or lighting will have to be certified. The rules will generally consist of practical rules that are designed to keep the studio and your cast and crew out of danger. Apart from the major risks that you could face if you don't follow the guidelines, minor infringements, such as smoking cigarettes on set, can result in your production being immediately shut down;

so it's a good idea to read the guidelines carefully and make sure your crew follows them.

Pros

Shooting in a studio environment is an amazing opportunity that can simplify the shooting process. Everything in and around the studio will be explicitly designed for the task of making films. Using a studio to shoot in is very much like having a blank canvas; if you have the means to create in it, then you can achieve almost anything you want.

Cons

The hire of the soundstage itself is often out of the reach of many short filmmakers. Having a blank canvas can literally mean buying a lot of paint to fill it.

When considering a studio of any size then you really need to have the budget to take advantage of it. You will need to also budget for everything else you'll require when using it, which often adds up to several times the actual hire fee. The soundstage will normally have to be insured for a minimum of £5,000,000 to £10,000,000. The other disadvantage is that the building of a set in a studio normally takes longer than shooting the scenes in or on it, so you'll need to hire the studio for the duration of the set build and take down, as well as the shot itself.

BUDGET SAVING

Film studios are designed for commercial filmmaking. They are intended for making feature films, adverts and television programmes. The rate card prices that studios will list will reflect the type of budgets that these productions have. They will typically quote per day or four-day week.

Like all filmmaking hire services they are faced with down time. Soundstages will often be unused for weeks or months a year in between productions. This is when you will have a chance of hiring a soundstage at a discounted rate. Explaining to the studio that you are a non-profit-making project on a tiny budget can potentially help you get terms that might be feasible for your film. If you can be flexible about when you shoot, you may well be able to hire a stage for a fraction of what a large production would have to pay.

Another strategy is to try and get as many services as you can thrown in; studios will often add in changing, hair and make up rooms at no extra cost if they are not being used.

There is, however, no such thing as shooting in a studio for free. Electric bills, catering and insurance will all need to be paid for even if you are paying little or nothing for hire.

10. INSURANCE

Organising insurance is going to be an essential requirement for your short film. Even if you are shooting a tiny scale project, if you are hiring equipment, using a location or studio, and the shoot involves cast and crew, then an insurance policy is mandatory. It's therefore crucial to the planning and budgeting of your film.

Insurance requirements vary from country to country, although they are often similar in nature and required for the same reasons. The following is a rough guide to insurance for film in the UK, the basics of when and why insurance might be needed. Different insurance brokers will have varying policies for different requirements.

You may find that your project can be made without needing insurance, but that is really only the case for micro productions that are made with borrowed equipment and have a cast and crew comprised of friends (who you are sure won't sue you if they get injured or worse).

Insurance for short films can seem quite complicated, but depending on the needs of the film, breaks down into three distinct areas.

TYPES OF INSURANCE

Employer's liability

If you are registering yourself as a company to make your film, or you are using an existing production company, then employer liability insurance is a statutory requirement (by law).

Employer's liability will cover the cast and crew working on your film. The standard policy limit minimum is £10,000,000. Although this is a huge figure, a policy for just a day or a week can be a feasible sum, but may still be a large proportion of your budget.

Public liability

If you are not a company and not officially employing anyone on your shoot you may not need employer's liability insurance. However, if you are planning on shooting in a hired interior or exterior location, or one that you need official permission to use, then you will require a public liability policy.

Public liability policies will cover you and your production against any injury or damage caused to third parties or property. For most location hire, proof of such a policy will be essential for you to be able to shoot there. For film studio hire this will be mandatory, with the studio setting the minimum cover you must provide, normally £5,000,000 to £10,000,000. Public liability insurance can be obtained for a day to a year depending on how long it's required for your film.

Equipment insurance

Equipment insurance will need to be provided for any professional equipment hired from rental companies. Professional camera and lighting equipment can be worth huge sums of money and the amount you will have to pay for insurance is directly proportional to the expense of the equipment you hire. The overall price of the equipment will need to be insured against damage, theft or loss.

Even when you're being loaned equipment for a discount rate or for free, you will still need insurance to be able to use it. Rental companies will not let equipment leave the premises without a copy of the insurance policy, and brokers will often need serial number information for the more expensive pieces of equipment such as cameras.

SMALL PRINT

Just because you have taken out one or all of these policies for your film, does not mean that you are covered in any event.

Insurance policies will have very stringent guidelines that must be adhered to. These guidelines can be as long as a small book, but you will need to read and understand the guidelines so that you are aware of the conditions under which the policy is valid.

You will also have to provide the insurers with accurate information about the specifics of your film. If you change any of these or do not adhere to their guidelines then your policy won't be valid. Breaking health and safety rules or suddenly deciding to involve pyrotechnics or stunts in your film can make the policy worthless. So always make sure that you provide accurate information as to the nature of your shoot and stay well within the policy rules.

WHERE TO GET SHORT FILM INSURANCE

You may be able to find standard insurance brokers that will have policies that might be applicable for your film but it can often be difficult to find the type of short-term policies that you will want for a short film. For this you will have to find a broker that deals purely with the entertainment industry, or has a specific department for entertainment insurance. The advantage of this is that you can often get a bespoke policy that is tailored to the requirements of your film and because of their experience with dealing with film productions they will often be able to offer you advice on the various policies you might need. The other advantage of the broker's experience is that they will be able and used to drawing up policies much faster than standard insurers. This is often essential for film shoots, where policies might need to be extended or modified days or even hours before the shoot.

Professional film databases will have contact details for insurance brokers that deal specifically with film projects.

Other insurance

It is possible to insure the negative if you are shooting on film, or tape stock if you are shooting on video. This will cover your film if the negative is exposed or damage occurs due to faulty camera equipment etc. This type of coverage will normally cover you for up to the limit of the budget of the entire production. This is only really worthwhile if your production has some major financial investment and is more typical on feature films.

BUDGET SAVING

Insurance, just like most other commodities involved in filmmaking, is negotiable.

Insurance companies work competitively against each other to try and entice as much business as possible. The amounts that you will have to insure for are often statutory requirements, or will be figures set by hire companies and studios to cover loss and damage of equipment or property. These figures are often non-negotiable; however, the amount you will have to pay to cover them may not be.

If you are organising insurance then always try to get quotes from as many different companies as possible. Make sure you inform other companies of the lowest quote you have had and see if they will give you a lower quote. Also check with equipment hire companies whether the amount they require you to insure their equipment for is insurable on an old for old policy or a new for old. An old for old policy will always be substantially cheaper to obtain as it covers the equipment for replacement with second hand gear rather than brand new.

11. SHORT FILM FORMATS

CHOOSING A FORMAT

The format that you shoot your film on is also known as the acquisition format or origination format, as this will often be different from the final format you screen your film on.

Choosing a format to shoot a short film on is not an easy task; what you may gain in ease of use and value you may lose in image quality and vice versa. Understanding not just the quality that various formats offer, but also what they entail as far as workflows go, is essential in making an informed decision.

There is no such thing as a best format, as all formats have their strengths and weaknesses. It's up to you to find the one that suits the style and budget of your film. Although a lot of importance is often placed on the formats that various short films are made on, it's important to remember that a good film doesn't rely on its means of production.

Which acquisition format you choose will probably be governed by your budget. When considering formats, you not only need to think about the costs of hiring the camera, whether video or film, and the stock you will need, but also the type of post-production workflows that the given format entails.

With a format such as MiniDV, the resulting workflow may be very straightforward, and the entire post-production could be completed on a home computer. Whereas shooting on film will entail not just the cost of the camera hire and stock, but also the costs of processing and transfer.

What acquisition format you choose should be carefully weighed up between the cost of the format and the quality it provides. The following is a

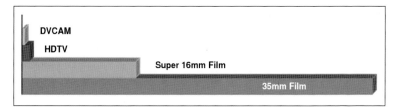

Figure 19. Costs of shooting on various formats.

basic list of commonly used formats for short films, in order of ascending quality.

- 35 MM
- S16 MM
- HD
- HDV
- DV

This refers to quality as in the resolution, colour space etc that each format is capable of producing in optimum circumstances. The quality of these formats is dependent on many variables, so this list assumes that each is used with the best equipment in the best conditions.

With so much choice and so many variables, the quality of formats is a subject of constant debate; certain aspects of any format may out-perform others and all formats are constantly being improved upon. So when choosing any format you should do your research to find which suits your film most.

EXPLOITING A FORMAT

In the spectrum of formats that are available to you as a filmmaker each has a set of characteristics and idiosyncrasies, which when taken advantage of can contribute to creating a specific look.

It is a common mistake for people to assume that just by choosing a particular format this will instantly produce a certain look that may be associated with it. When making your choice, it's always important to remember that higher quality is only useful if you have the means to exploit its potential.

Most people will be aware of the difference in, say, the visual qualities of footage shot on MiniDV, compared to that of footage shot on 35mm film. On a very basic level they look different because of the amount of visual information that each is capable of recording (see resolution), with MiniDV being at the low end and 35mm at the high end. But when considering how you want your film to look it is important to remember that what you may associate with MiniDV video footage and 35mm film footage is probably dependent on examples you have already seen.

Most people will have had experience with a video camera set on an auto pre-set and associate this basic look with the format. You might also associate films seen at the cinema with 35mm. In terms of quality of resolution that each is capable of recording, it is certainly true that one is of extremely superior quality to the other, but to assume that to shoot your film on video will give it the look of a bad wedding video and to shoot on 35mm will make it look just like a Hollywood movie is not true.

One of the reasons why so much video footage looks low-quality and 35mm looks high is to do with the conditions in which they are used. Video cameras, due to their size and price, are ubiquitous and used in all kinds of different situations, whereas 35mm cameras, due to their size and price, are rarely used outside the controlled environments of commercial filmmaking. What I mean here by controlled environments is studio or location set ups, where it is common practice to adjust every detail to define the look of the shot. This can range from the lighting, which could have taken hours or even days to be set up, right down to the shades of a character's costume or make up, chosen due to the speed of the film stock being used. This kind of attention to detail goes a long way to producing the look of a lot of films shot on 35mm and therefore the image we generally associate with it. I'm not saying that if you were to recreate this level of control for a video shoot the image would be as good as film, as it wouldn't even come close, it just doesn't have the capability. However, controlling as many factors as you can when using any format will allow you to achieve much better quality and unity in the images you are capturing. When used under these controlled circumstances you may well be surprised how lower resolution formats will out-perform your initial expectations.

If your deciding factor over which format to use is budget, which it normally is, you will sometimes find yourself on the borderline between being able to afford a higher-resolution format and a lower one. Always consider the pros and cons carefully. Although it is common practice for filmmakers to strive for the better quality format, consider what else you could spend the extra budget on that may not improve the resolution but could improve the production values in other ways. Obvious examples like lighting, set design and costumes can make a massive difference in the film's look and it just might be worth compromising on the image quality to make the overall appearance of the film more unique.

ASPECT RATIO

Aspect ratio is a term used to refer to the dimensions of an image. It is specified as a ratio that relates to the height in comparison to the width rather than a measurement in cm or inches, as these measurements will vary depending on the size of a monitor or projection screen, while the aspect ratio governs the shape.

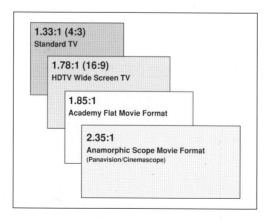

Figure 20. Common aspect ratios.

Aspect ratios are used to describe the dimension of all kinds of images within filmmaking, from projected cinema images to the shape of a viewfinder. The figures are derived by dividing the width of the image by its height. This can then be expressed in a number of ways. In filmmaking the height of the image is normally given as 1.

This creates common aspect ratios such as 1.66:1 for the dimensions of a Super 16mm film image or 1.33:1 for a 35mm film image. However, using 1 as a constant isn't a standard outside of filmmaking. So many aspect ratios for television and video formats are given as ratios to other figures. For example standard televisions and computer monitors have an aspect ratio expressed as 4:3, while widescreen HDTV iSuper is 16:9. This disparity in how aspect ratios are expressed can be confusing. Image sizes that are very similar can have seemingly very different ratios attached to them.

For instance Super 16mm film with its aspect ratio of 1.66:1 is nearly the same ratio as HDTV 16:9, which is why Super 16 is very suitable for HDTV broadcast.

Widescreen

Due to the current switch from standard-definition television to high-definition, the old 4:3 aspect ratio is gradually being phased out in favour of the high-definition 16:9 aspect ratio. This is an important consideration when choosing what aspect ratio to shoot and screen your film in, as most broadcasting channels no longer accept 4:3 SD for broadcast.

Masking/letterboxing

It is common practice when making a film to start with the largest aspect ratio you can. Many 35mm films are shot at academy 1.33:1, which is nearly the same as 4:3. However, only the central part of the image is used, so that it ends up having an aspect ratio of 1.85:1, which is a widescreen format. This is achieved by the rest of the image being masked out with black strips, referred to as letterboxing or postboxing.

Racking

When an image has been captured at a larger or different-sized aspect ratio than that which it will be screened at, the result is extra frame area that will eventually be masked out. This extra frame area can be moved up or down, before the masking is applied, allowing the image to be reframed during editing or conforming.

Pan and scan

Pan and scan is a process used to display widescreen images on ordinary 4:3 displays such as standard television. Rather than letterboxing the image, which allows the whole frame to be seen, pan and scan only shows a portion of the widescreen image. It is common practice for widescreen features to undergo a pan and scan for broadcast on television. The process of scanning only a portion of the frame and then panning to another area can also be used as a creative technique during post-production.

12. VIDEO

Video is a long-established format for shooting short films on. The availability and low cost of shooting on video has led to a whole new generation
of filmmakers who might never otherwise have had the budget to get into
filmmaking.

The advent and development of video technology has lent itself perfectly to
the needs of short filmmakers and while it used to be synonymous with bad
image quality and low production standards, the technology has advanced
massively over the last decade, resulting in new higher-definition formats and
an improvement in quality for even the most basic of video cameras. New
video formats are emerging yearly and increasing the quality available to the
filmmaker. Where video used to be associated with a certain look and style,
new high-definition formats are much closer to the look of film. Technology
that five years ago was only available to a select few Hollywood directors
has filtered down into the prosumer market and is now widely available to
many short filmmakers. The digital revolution will continue advancing at high
speed, and it's only a matter of time before domestic video cameras will offer these same cinema-quality images, democratising the technical side of
the filmmaking process. For the moment, however, there is a huge difference
between different types of video formats and the quality they offer. To differentiate between them you need to be able to understand the fundamental
differences, and then work out which one is right for you and your film.

Analogue

Analogue used to be the predominant way in which video information was
recorded and played back before digital surpassed it. There are still many

analogue video formats in use that offer high quality. However, the major drawback with analogue formats is that each time footage is played back, or a transfer is made, degradation and loss of information is more likely to occur and this is what makes digital preferable. Unless you don't have any digital options there is really not much point in using an analogue video format anymore. Filmmaking has for some time been geared towards digital workflows, so choosing an analogue format will make your workflow options more complicated, with digitisation required to convert the analogue information.

Digital

Digital video stores image and sound information by sampling frequencies and then transforms this information into numbers known as bits and bytes which create binary codes. This method of information storage is very stable, allowing transfers to be made quickly, through multiple generations, with little or no loss of quality. Digital video has revolutionised filmmaking and, apart from processes involving film negatives and prints, filmmaking has largely converted entirely to digital formats and systems. This has produced more and more compatibility between systems such as digital cameras and editing suites. Coupled with the speed at which digital technology works, this means that workflows are now becoming simpler, and enables very immediate results. For instance, plugging a digital video camera straight into a computer with a firewire to transfer the footage is entirely based on digital technology.

Compression

The amount of digital information needed to create a video image is huge, and, for it to be storable or transferable on most digital tape formats, compression is needed. What compression does is take the digital information for an image and convert it into more efficient and feasible amounts. Digital compression achieves this by encoding the digital data through the use of codecs. This encoded information results in smaller files so that more can be stored and transferred, for example, onto a digital tape or computer hard drive. Once at its required destination, generally a computer hard drive, the information can be decompressed and played back. The most important thing to understand with this process is that, although there are many varieties of compression and ways of performing compression, they all fall into two main categories, lossless or lossy.

Lossless is a form of compression that results in the decompressed files retaining all the original information and therefore quality that they had before they were compressed. Lossless compression is ideal for filmmakers as the original quality of the image is preserved. The drawback, however, is that high-quality uncompressed footage returns to its large file sizes and so requires huge amounts of storage and high processing speeds to work with.

Lossy compression by its nature needs to reduce the amount of information that an image contains. Given the characteristics of any moving image, there are several different aspects of it that the codec can reduce; colour information, size and resolution, and sound can all be compressed, but how many codecs achieve compression is by literally throwing information away. This is not as drastic as it may sound. If you imagine most digital cameras are capable of capturing images with millions of colours in, much of the colour detail will actually be imperceptible to the human eye. So, for example, a certain form of compression might potentially operate by deciding which ranges are not as important as others and get rid of the ones not needed. This may result in an image that looks the same as the original image, but will have slightly less subtlety in the range of colours. In general, high-resolution images always contain more detail than you can actually see, so compression codecs are generally based on the principle that they lose the less pertinent information. This resulting lack of detail may be imperceptible unless you want to perform processes such as grading, which will change the original emphasis of apparent colours and relies on there being high amounts of colour information. Images that will later be blown up for projection will also often expose the detail lost during compression. Sound on the other hand, due to its reasonably small file sizes, rarely needs to be compressed. Lossy compression is generally a necessary evil as uncompressed footage is often impossible to store and process. It allows us to record, store and process larger amounts and is ubiquitous within digital filmmaking. This then presents the filmmaker with a choice over how much information is lost and of what kind. Different formats employ different codecs using different amounts and types of compression and this should inform the filmmaker's choice of which format to choose.

Bad compression

It's a common misconception for people to think that choosing a format with the least compression gives them the best quality. What's important to remember is that high-resolution formats often require more compression than lower ones, simply because there's more data to capture. For instance, a format with four times more data information than another might employ twice as much compression, but at the end of the day it has four times more data that has been compressed so will be far better quality than the low data that has only been lightly compressed.

RESOLUTION

Resolution is a term used to describe video image quality. It refers to how much detail an image contains and therefore its sharpness. It is widely used when describing the specifications of any technology that deals with image acquisition, storage, transfer or display.

Resolution is normally expressed in either numbers of lines or numbers of pixels and used to describe digital and analogue images alike.

Having a basic understanding of the resolution of different formats will be extremely useful to you because the image quality of your film will depend on which format you choose for acquisition and how you maintain that resolution through your post-production workflow. Although the technical specifications of formats can seem rather daunting to the novice, gaining understanding of how resolution and quality is described will be essential to you as a filmmaker.

Lines

Resolution within most filmmaking processes will be referred to in lines of resolution, generally in lines per image size, rather than per mm or inch. This is because the image size of a format can vary; television screens vary in size and so do projected images, whilst still containing the same image specifications. The amount of lines an image consists of is also not dependent on its aspect ratio.

In the simplest terms video images of any format are constructed from a tight weave of black and white lines that respond to input signals to create images. The tighter the weave of lines the sharper the image will be. A tighter weave needs more lines running both horizontally and vertically to create it.

An easy way to look at resolution lines is that the more of them there are the higher the image quality will be. This means that there are going to be two figures that affect an image's resolution, the number of lines running horizontally and the number of lines running vertically.

However, the amount of vertical lines that an image contains is fixed according to format and cannot change; it is only the amount of horizontal lines that can fluctuate.

So for example, two digital video cameras of the same format will have the same amount of vertical lines per image, but one may offer higher quality because it has more horizontal lines, therefore more pixels and so a higher resolution.

In television broadcast the lines involved are often a greater number than the ones that actually make up the image, so for instance a standard-definition NTSC TV image would contain 525 lines yet only 480 would make up the picture, as the rest of the lines are used to store information and so are not active.

Pixels

If you imagine that the lines of an image are forming a weave of horizontal and vertical lines, then the tiny squares that this creates are referred to as pixels.

Some image resolutions are given just as pixels or in pixels per image size. These figures are often expressed in Mega pixels, which is a figure calculated by multiplying the number of vertical lines by the horizontal lines and dividing by one million.

Why use a higher resolution?

Higher resolutions give sharper, clearer pictures that lend themselves better to being blown up in size via projection. Because filmmaking involves so many different stages, it is often not possible to record, edit and screen video images at the same resolution.

It's common for video cameras to offer capture resolutions greater than the resolution of the format they will be recorded on, or for television series that will only be displayed at standard TV resolution to be shot on 35mm film. This opens up the obvious question of why use a higher-resolution format if the final display resolution will be much lower? When a higher resolution is down converted to a lower one, much of the initial visual quality is captured, even though the resolution will be no different; the quality of an image shot on 35mm and then put onto MiniDV will look much higher in quality than an image shot on a DV camera although they will still be the same resolution.

PAL/NTSC

PAL and NTSC are two types of television broadcast systems. Although technically a type of colour encoding, they are broadly used to describe the line resolutions that each of them use: PAL images being 720 x 625 and NTSC 720 x 525, with PAL running at 25 frames, 50 fields a second and NTSC at 30 frames, 60 fields a second. NTSC has been the North American format and PAL the European. Although this technology is being phased out by HD it's important to bear in mind that the two don't really mix. So if you're sending a copy of your film to a festival abroad or using a camera from another country, it's important to check whether you are dealing with PAL or NTSC.

STANDARD-DEFINITION (SD)/SDTV

Standard-definition refers to a standard resolution for broadcasting and video capture formats, regardless of aspect ratio. This is an important point to bear in mind; just because an image has a 16:9 widescreen aspect ratio it doesn't mean that it is necessarily high-definition.

Conventionally, standard-definition has been the standard for all digital video formats and for digital television broadcast, normally with a 4:3 aspect ratio and a resolution of PAL 720 x 625 (576 active) or NTSC 720 x 525 (480 active).

HIGH-DEFINITION (HD)/HDTV

High-definition is a higher-resolution format that has begun to supersede standard-definition, both as a digital broadcast standard and as a digital video format in its own right. It offers a huge leap in resolution quality, with almost four times the resolution of SD. Although only a few channels offer HD broadcast at the present time the entire film and television industry is on the verge of switching over to purely high-definition environments with the majority of productions now being shot and post-produced on an HD format even if they are still broadcast at SD. This means that everything from cameras to tapes to televisions are changing from the old SD format to the new HD format and once this has happened SD will be obsolete. Because this is a relatively new technology there are currently several versions of HD resolution and a fair amount of confusion over which is true HD. Currently HD is split between the options of 1280 x 720 or 1920 x 1080. Both are HD formats and many television channels will broadcast both. Digital cameras and tapes also offer one or both of these variations. To complicate matters further another factor is how these resolutions are scanned.

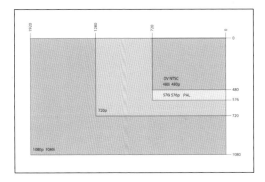

Figure 21.
Common resolutions, courtesy of www.wikipedia.org

Interlaced scanning

Interlaced scanning is a process that was devised for broadcast of television images. It works by splitting a single frame of an image into two fields, with odd and even lines making up each. In a sense each one is only really half the image and each half image is interlaced with the next to create the whole until it is refreshed with the next two half fields. With NTSC the picture is refreshed 30 times a second giving 60 half fields, and with PAL 25 times a second giving 50 half fields. These are referred to as 60i and 50i. Although interlaced scanning has provided a valuable method for video and television capture and broadcast for a long time, the disadvantages such as the jagged edges and poor image quality have not made it ideal for filmmaking.

Progressive scanning

Progressive scanning is a newer concept that offers greater image quality by scanning complete fields from top to bottom instead of the half fields generated with interlaced. With progressive scanning in NTSC, 30 whole frames are generated a second and with PAL, 25 frames a second, also referred to as 30p and 25p.

24/25P

Apart from the potential image quality problems associated with interlaced scanning, the reason why progressive scan technology is so appealing to filmmakers is that 24 or 25 frames a second is exactly the same rate that film cameras and projectors capture and project films. 24/25 frame rates have a very specific visual quality that we associate with film, and watching video at this scan rate gives a film feel to the images. By adding only five or six more frames to take it up to an NTSC frame rate, the image gains a very different quality that we associate with television and video rather than film.

The first cameras to start capturing 24p images were developed by George Lucas, in an attempt to develop a video image that behaved like film. This technology has spread and has been available in prosumer cameras. There is also a version of 24p known as cineframe. This is not true 24p, it merely gives a similar visual effect and is found on many prosumer and domestic video camera ranges. HDTV broadcast also gives various options on receiving interlaced or progressive images.

1080p/1080i/720p

These are all HD resolutions with interlaced or progressive scans. At present these are the main three options that are offered in most HD technology, whether cameras or monitors. One of the problems with progressive scanning is that because it is generated from full frames rather than half fields, it requires larger files to be generated much faster. This is particularly a problem for video camera technology where the tape formats that have been viable for SD video are not really capable of handling HD progressive resolutions. As a result many current video cameras offer a variety of HD solutions, so 1080 interlaced or 720 progressive, often with a choice between them in a single camera. 1080 progressive is regarded as true HD and is the ideal for most filmmakers. It is also becoming available as an option in prosumer cameras that record straight to disc or storage cards as well as professional cameras that record to disc or very high-resolution tape formats.

As disconcerting as so many options can be, the bottom line for the moment is that they are all HD formats and look much, much better than standard-definition video. Ultimately it's a trade-off between quality and practicality: what you lose in quality you might gain in ease and speed of use.

HDV

HDV is a technology offered by various video manufacturers that records HD resolution images onto DV or MiniDV tapes using MPEG2 Gop (group of images) compression. Because HD images are so high in data compared to DV, more compression is used to encode the images onto the small tapes. So although HDV technology technically offers much higher-resolution images, the images are far more compressed than standard-definition video captured on DV. However, the overall amount of data with HDV is far higher that SD video. Gop compression works by not recording every frame completely, just key frames, and then recreating the frames in between those from highly compressed data. This recreation process often occurs when capturing the footage onto a computer-based editing system, for example.

COLOUR SPACE/SAMPLING

The colour information or colour space of most video images is recorded by using varying intensities of red, green and blue (RGB) information. Three separate channels record intensities of the individual RGB information and then they are combined, making it possible to approximately recreate any colour that the camera picks up. The problem with RGB colour space is that the amount of information generated for the three different channels of colour is huge, so again, as with most digital video formats, this needs to be compressed to fit onto a tape or easily transferred. For this, most digital formats use chroma subsampling. With subsampling the RGB data is transferred into three components, but instead of them being three colour channels like RGB, the first of these components is a luminance (luma) and the other two are chrominance (chroma). Luma is the light and dark information and chroma is the colour information. Subsampling reduces the RGB data by preferencing the way the human eye actually sees; the eye is much more sensitive to luminance than it is to colour, so with subsampling there is always the full amount of luma data and then often much smaller amounts of the two chroma datas. In digital video, the three amounts of data of the three components are expressed with figures such as 4:2:0 or 4:1:1. The first figure is the luma, with 4 being the full data and 1 being a quarter of the full data. So for instance with 4:1:1, the two chroma figures after the luma have only a quarter of the amount of data as the luma. This is not necessarily as drastic as it may sound, with the image still looking convincing to the eye, but consisting of far less data than an RGB image. Without needing to understand the intricacies of colour space data, you can use these numbers as a guide to see how much colour information a format offers. Colour space is extremely important for high-end filmmaking, with processes like grading or chroma key effects relying heavily on the need for as much colour info as possible and, as you will see, different formats offer vastly different amounts.

VIDEO CAMERAS

Video cameras work on the same principle as film cameras, but instead of the light absorbed through the lens being channelled onto light-sensitive film it is channelled onto a light-sensitive chip or chips. These chips then convert the light information into electrical signals. Cameras designed to record a certain format of digital video such as DV or HDV often vary in quality through the features they offer. The type of lens, light sensitivity and amount of chips all affect the quality of the images they capture regardless of what format it is in.

Monitoring

One of the great advantages of shooting on video is that you can actually see the images you are getting as you record them. Although most video cameras offer LCD view finders and additional flip screens, both of these, due to their size, often don't allow the user to see more than enough detail to judge composition and framing. To judge image information such as brightness and contrast more accurately, the video camera is normally hooked up to a field monitor, which is large enough to give sufficient information, but still feasible to move around on location.

CCD chips

CCD is the general type of chip used in video cameras; their size and shape is directly linked to the quality and shape of the image they produce. Domestic video cameras tend to just use a quarter inch CCD chip, while prosumer cameras will use 1/3 inch chips and professional cameras use 2/3 inch chips.

The higher-quality cameras will also use three chips rather than just a single chip, recording more information by splitting the light beam into red, green and blue and sending that information to an individual chip. The actual shape of the chip will also determine the aspect ratio of the image with standard-definition chips recording a 4:3 aspect ratio and high-definition cameras recording a 16:9 aspect ratio. New video cameras are also beginning to use CMOS chips, which are larger and more sensitive than CCD chips.

Tapeless

The first generation of cameras to bypass tapes completely has arrived. Storage cards that could only store small standard-definition video images have now been developed to capture large high-definition video. Portable hard drives are also being used instead of tape formats, allowing pure digital file workflows at very high resolutions. This will only continue in the future with videotapes becoming obsolete.

Figure 22.
Panasonic HVX200 records straight to P2 memory cards or fire store hard drive, eliminating the need for tapes, courtesy of Panasonic.

VIDEO THAT LOOKS LIKE FILM

Video has always had a certain look associated with it that is different to film, both in quality and feel. As discussed, the main factors that have differentiated film from video have been frame rate, resolution, colour space and shallow depth of field. Despite numerous attempts at filmising video throughout the years, one or more of these factors has always meant that the results have been unconvincing.

In the last few years, however, HD has meant that video footage has obtained nearly all the qualities of film. Though still a long way from the resolution of 35mm, HD resolution cameras using progressive scanning technology have closed the gap considerably. Until recently the technology involved had been reserved for cameras that, due to their cost and demand, remained purely in the professional domain. Now ranges of prosumer cameras are starting to appear in the market that offer the same quality; while still expensive, they are nowhere near the price of the pro cameras. The HD capability of these cameras, coupled with developments such as the 35mm lens adapters (see lenses), means it is now possible for short filmmakers to shoot video that potentially rivals the look and feel of film for a fraction of the cost.

The final hurdle for independent filmmakers to compete with the technical quality of big-budget features really remains in the screening of these films. Films screened from 35mm prints have always been far better quality than any type of video projection. This has been a stumbling block for most filmmakers who don't have the amount of money needed to create a 35mm print. Standard-definition video, because of its low resolution, might look fairly good on a small screen, but when blown up to cinema screen size typically looks quite poor in comparison with film. But with the advent of digital film workflows and technology, cinemas are beginning to take the first steps into transferring to high-resolution digital projections. Films can then play from hard discs and digital tapes with outstanding results. Inevitably this will become the standard screening method for new films, offering independent filmmakers the possibility of producing incredible quality films on tiny budgets.

DIGITAL VIDEO FORMATS AND TAPES

Video formats are often confusing, with manufacturers introducing variations of tape for a single format. Cameras for those formats in turn offer their own unique strong and weak points, all of which affect the quality of the footage you can record with them.

DV

DV is a standard-definition format recorded onto DV tapes either mini or standard size. There are three main types of DV tape available within the format.

- DV
- DVCAM
- DVCPRO 25/50

DVCAM and DVCPRO are professional versions of DV and offer faster tape speeds resulting in more reliable capture and playback, as well as improved colour space compared to standard DV. They are, however, all DV, so they use the same codec to capture and store the data and all have the same resolution. This format is widely available; cameras can be bought or hired comparatively cheaply.

- Resolution: 720 x 576 in PAL or 720 x 420 in NTSC.
- Sampling: 4:1:1 or 4:2:0 depending on PAL or NTSC and tape type.

Figure 23.
Sony PD150 DV Three chip DV camera, courtesy of SONY.

HDV

HDV, as discussed above, is an HD resolution format that records onto DV tapes. It produces Super 16 x 9 aspect ratio images and although highly compressed has dramatically greater resolutions than standard-definition. Apart from recording onto all the standard DV tapes, there is also a DVCPRO HD tape designed specifically for HDV. True 1080p cannot be recorded onto DV tapes, so the cameras on the market offer either 1080i or 720p options, many of them giving the option of recording both, as well as standard-definition too. HDV technology is found in a variety of prosumer cameras that, although more expensive than most DV cameras, offer significant improvements in quality and versatility.

- Resolution: 1440 x 1080i or 1280 x 720p, various cameras offer 24/25p options.
- Sampling: 4:2:0.

Figure 24.
JVC HD101 HDV camera,
courtesy of JVC.

DIGITAL BETACAM (Digibeta)

Digibeta is a professional standard-definition format. It's widely used throughout both the film and television industries and is the highest quality standard-definition format available. Despite their quality and reliability, Digibeta cameras and technology are extremely expensive to either purchase or hire. Digibeta tapes remain the standard for mastering many short films to, and is also the standard video format for screening at film festivals.

Figure 25.
Sony DVW-970P Digital
betacam camera, courtesy
of SONY.

- Resolution: 720 x 576 in PAL or 720 x 420 in NTSC.
- Sampling: 4:2:2.

HD

HD is the highest resolution video format available. Similar to DV, manufacturers offer different tape formats of varying quality. Currently available are:

- HDCAM
- HDCAM-SR
- HDCAM-D5

HD is often recorded straight to a hard drive, bypassing the need for tape completely, which means the images don't have to be compressed.

With its amazingly high-resolution and colour sampling, HD is as close to film as video gets. With more and more feature films being shot on it all the time, it is ideal for filmmaking. The drawback for short filmmakers, however, has been that the cameras and tapes used to record HD have been very expensive to rent; often it has been cheaper to shoot on film formats like 16mm. This is beginning to change, and the first prosumer cameras that offer true 1080p resolution are now arriving on the market for the same price as other HDV and SD cameras. These cameras record directly to hard drives or removable storage cards, and will have a huge impact on the quality of low-budget filmmaking.

Figure 26.
Sony HD XDCAM,
courtesy of SONY.

- Resolution: 1920 x 1080p or 1920 x 1080i or 1280 x 720p, various cameras offer 24/25p as well as variable frame rates.
- Sampling: 4:4:2 or 4:4:4 depending on tape or straight to disc options.

CHOOSING A CAMERA

Once you have chosen a format to shoot on, you also need to choose a camera. If you have a DP, they will normally be instrumental in making a decision; if not it will be up to you.

Within each format and market type – domestic, prosumer and professional – you will find a massive variety of cameras on offer by different manufacturers. Often there is not a huge amount of difference between those of the same formats. The most important choice, therefore, is one of functionality. You need to choose a camera that you or your DP feels comfortable working with, that will be conducive to creativity.

The amount and type of connections a camera has can also make a huge difference to the workflow of your film. Cameras that offer digital in and outs can potentially save you hours of transfer time or VTR deck hire, giving you the simple and efficient ability to dock the camera to your editing computer for transfer of rushes and outputting of your finished film back onto the same format. Cameras with XLR sockets will also allow you to record multiple sound sources from different microphones.

SHOOTING ON VIDEO

Although the great advantage of shooting on video is the freedom that cheap, hour-long tapes give you, there is much to be learnt from the protocols developed for shooting on film (see structure of shooting on film). Slating and logging takes, combined with a defined order for each take, will generally produce much better results and make the rest of your workflow considerably easier. Just as with shooting on film, the defining factor for how good an image looks is lighting.

13. FILM

Shooting on film, whether Super 16mm or 35mm, you are not only ben-efiting from two of the highest resolution formats, but also technology that has been designed for the sole purpose of filmmaking. Whereas shooting on video gives instant results, shooting on film requires multiple processes, such as development of the negative and transfer onto a video format, before you can begin post-production. Films are no longer made just on film. The advent of computer-based editing systems has meant that film is really only used for acquisition and projection, with the rest of the workflow taking place on digital computer-based systems. It's becoming increasingly rare that the original negative is used at all after transfer, and it's now possible to carry out extremely high-resolution Digital Intermediates.

WHY SHOOT ON FILM?

Despite the ever-increasing quality and resolution of digital formats they still can't rival the quality of film. Both 16mm and 35mm are still way ahead which is what makes it so desirable to shoot films on these formats. With over a hundred years of trial and development, film stocks are still evolving and producing better and better results. The way that the film is handled in post-production has switched almost exclusively to digital, but film itself is still the shooting format of choice for any production that can handle the substantial costs.

There are two main components to shooting on film, one being the film stock, the other being the camera. It's useful to have at least a basic knowl-edge of both of these and it will help you understand why using film demands a different protocol than using a digital format. Many people who have used film-based stills cameras will be familiar with much of the following, which is a basic guide to how film stock and film cameras function. This is essential knowledge for anyone who is contemplating using film.

FILM STOCK

Unlike digital images, where the image is created from thousands of small pixels of colour and contrast information, film records an image through the use of layers of light-sensitive grains, which react to record colour and contrast. It is the consistency of its structure that allows film to surpass the quality of images that are created with pixels.

Modern film stocks are essentially a strip of plastic that is coated on one side with a light-sensitive emulsion. When correctly exposed to a light source, the silver halides in the emulsion react to form an image. This image can then be revealed through further chemical processing, referred to as developing. At this stage a positive print can be made from the negative or the negative can be transferred to a digital format (see telecine and DI). The exception to this is reversal stock that creates a positive image at the developing stage; however, reversal stock is not commonly used in filmmaking.

Gauges

Film gauges are normally referred to by the actual width of the stock. So 35mm, 16mm and 8mm refer to the actual measurements of one single frame. Film stocks are perforated on one or both edges, which allows the camera mechanism to physically pull the film through the camera.

Lengths

Conventional film stocks are available in various standardised lengths, normally 100ft, 400ft or 1,000ft lengths. For both 16mm and 35mm the most commonly used is 400ft. Apart from 100ft rolls that normally come in plastic cartridges, all other lengths come in tins, in which the film is stored in a light-proof bag and wrapped round a plastic core that fits directly into the camera magazine.

Apart from gauge and length, the differentiating factor between most film stocks is what is known as its speed. The speed of a film stock refers to its sensitivity to light and this is known as its ASA. Different film stocks are designed to be more or less sensitive to various amounts and types of light. Certain stocks are therefore chosen due to their suitability for the lighting conditions in which they will be used. On a simplified level, faster stocks (more light-sensitive) are chosen for conditions where there is less light available. Whereas slower stocks (less light-sensitive) are chosen for conditions where there is an abundance of light. Various speeds of stock can produce different qualities in the image that is produced. Faster stocks are associated with a grainier image.

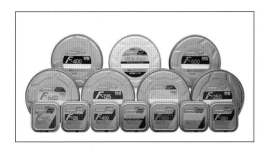

Figure 27.
Rolls of 400 and 1,000ft Fuji motion film stock, courtesy of FUJI.

Daylight/tungsten

Motion film stocks fall into two categories when it comes to the types of light they are designed for: daylight or tungsten light. These two stocks are chemically balanced to produce a realistic looking image when used in either daylight or with tungsten filament lights. The light produced from different sources has a different colour temperature when recorded on film and can result in a warmer or colder image (see lighting section). This altering of the colour balance is rectified by choosing the appropriate stock. Daylight or tungsten stocks can be used in either circumstances, so it is possible to shoot with the same stock in natural light conditions as well as artificial;

however, the balance needs to be rectified through use of gels on the light sources or filters on the camera lens.

On film stocks, tungsten and daylight are abbreviated to T or D, which is suffixed at the end of the ASA rating of the stock. So for example 500T refers to a stock that is designed to be fast and used in artificial light, whereas 100D refers to a slower stock for natural light situations. Stocks are often referred to by generic code numbers, which correlate to both the ASA and type of light it is designed for.

Colour/black and white

Stocks are also available in black and white or colour. Due to the diminishing use of black and white stocks they are generally not available in the same range of ASA ratings that colour film is. Although it is possible to use a colour stock to film with and then convert the image to monochrome at a later stage, black and white stock will generally produce images with more clarity and contrast than a converted colour image.

FILM CAMERAS

To explain the functions of the film camera it is necessary to differentiate between the lenses and the camera body. On an extremely basic level the film

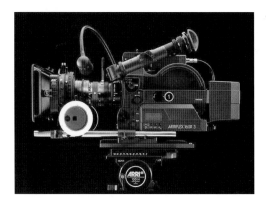

Figure 28.
Arri SR III Super 16mm camera, courtesy of Arri Group.

camera body's primary function is to pull the film stock through the camera while positioning it momentarily in front of a small aperture that corresponds to the diameter of the film stock.

This is a very simplified overview of film cameras, but it helps in realising how they function. All film cameras perform this task in different ways and to varying degrees of sophistication. Film cameras have advanced a long way from the early hand-cranked models, but the majority of advancements in image quality are due largely to improvements in film stock and lens quality, which means that a film camera is only as good as the lenses you put on it and the film stock that goes through it. However, modern cameras will offer a variety of features that make them more functional and provide more creative opportunities.

Sound

Although it may seem obvious to most, it's worth pointing out here that film cameras, whether Super 16 or 35mm, do not record sound. If you are going to shoot on film then you will need to record sound onto a sound recorder that is separate from the camera and stock. Any sound that you record will have to be synced to the footage after the shoot.

Magazines

Rather than load the film directly into the camera body, modern cameras will have detachable magazines. They are generally slotted on and off the camera simply and efficiently. Several magazines are normally provided when hiring a film camera, allowing them to be loaded with film away from the camera by an assistant, then quickly replaced when the film runs out.

Frame rate

Cameras will normally have a standard fixed-frame rate of 24 or 25 frames per second (FPS). This produces a normal speed image in which actions and movements occur at the same speed as they do in reality.

As well as these standard film camera frame rates, many cameras will have adjustable speeds, which allows the camera to achieve various frame rates, ranging from low frame rates that produce a speeded up image or high frame rates that produce a slow-motion image.

Standard cameras will offer frame rates that will range from 1 to 75 frames per second and modern cameras will allow you to ramp up and down between the speeds during a shot, producing fluctuations in the speed of movement captured.

For extreme slow motion, high-speed cameras are needed that can achieve frame rates of over 150 FPS.

Although most cameras will offer fixed-frame rates of 24/25 FPS, many older cameras will not have this as a constant speed. This means that these cameras are not viable for syncing sound recordings to and are only useful for silent filmmaking.

Video tap/video assist

On modern cameras it is possible to attach a video tap, which in turn can be connected to a video monitor, allowing you to see the image you are filming through the camera lens, without having to look through the eyepiece of the camera. The images produced by video taps do not give a real indication of the light or quality of the image that will be recorded on the film. However, it does allow you to make judgements about framing, lenses and camera moves.

Noise

Cameras make noise while running. Contemporary cameras will run almost silently, but even the small noise levels that they give off can cause problems when the camera is very close to the action being recorded. Audible camera noise that is picked up in the sound recording is usually overcome by 'blimping' the camera with a 'barney'. This is a padded cover placed over the camera to dampen any noise that might be emanating from it.

Older cameras, or cameras running at high speeds, will often make serious noise levels, which means that they are not feasible for shooting certain scenes or types of film with.

STRUCTURE OF SHOOTING ON FILM

The DP would normally be responsible for choosing a camera to fit both the needs of the film and your budget. As well as choosing the right stocks for the lighting conditions and looks you are trying to produce.

Loading

The unexposed film is loaded into several magazines by the clapper loader. Due to film's light-sensitive qualities, this is performed by placing both camera magazine and roll of film stock into a light-proof bag (change bag). The magazine is only removed once the loading is complete. The magazines are then labelled and numbered with the type and length of stock they contain.

A full magazine will be placed on the camera. The DP and assistants will set the frame rate of the camera and set the exposure according to the light meter readings for that shot. Focus will be measured and adjusted accordingly. These settings are logged by the clapper loader, both on a camera sheet and on the clapperboard (slate).

Slate/clapperboard

Slating is vital when shooting on film. It provides two key functions. First, it allows a visual record of the take number, and scene number, crucial for editing and transfer. Second, it generates time code, so the actual snap of the clapper against the board is the only reference for syncing the audio (recorded separately) with the film. Camera sheets are also kept as records of all camera info for each individual take.

Figure 29. Clapperboard being held in frame.

Commands

Once the camera is ready and the clapperboard filled in, the camera crew are ready.

The director or AD is then free to give the command 'roll camera' or 'turn over' and the DP or assistant starts the camera. The camera does not instantaneously reach the desired frame rate so there is a delay until it hits a constant speed. When a light signals this, the assistant will call out 'speed' or 'camera rolling'. At this point the clapper loader places the slate in front of the camera and says the take and scene number. The director is then free to say 'action' allowing the scene to commence.

When the take is finished, the command 'cut' is given, at which point the camera is stopped and the assistant will say 'camera cut'. The length of film that has been used in that take will be noted by the clapper loader, so the camera crew will know how much film is left for the next take. When the magazine has no, or little, unexposed film left inside, it is replaced and the process starts over again.

PROCESSING

At the end of the shoot or the end of that day's shoot, the film stock will be marked with the relevant information and, together with the camera sheets, will be dropped off at a film lab. This is then processed overnight and transferred onto various video formats via telecine, producing dailies or rushes ready for the production staff to watch, or scanned onto a hard drive.

Film processing and transfer is charged by the foot, except for a process such as grading, which is often charged by the hour.

SCREENING PRINTS

35mm prints are the favoured format for the screening of any films in a cinema projection environment. 16mm prints can also be screened at many festivals, but prints can only be screened on standard 16mm not Super 16mm; because Super 16mm uses the extra width of the film that would normally hold the magnetic audio track and perforations, it can't be projected with a soundtrack, so standard 16mm with it 4:3 aspect ratio is the only form of 16mm screening print.

The creation of 35mm screening prints is a complicated procedure that takes place at a film lab. Films that have been shot on 35mm are usually edited from video transfers to produce an EDL. This EDL is then given to the neg cutter at the lab who reassembles the edit using the frame and roll time code references from the EDL. Any elements of the finished film that do not appear on the original negative such as effects, titles and credits have to be optically transferred onto a 35mm negative and spliced into the master negative.

Once the neg has been cut and spliced together, an initial positive print is made, referred to as a work print or mute print. From a screening of this at the lab, a fine tuning of grading or colour timing can be decided, with subsequent work prints then generated until it is a close as possible to the desired look. The next print produced and screened is a trial print, complete with the magnetic soundtrack strip that is created by the lab from the audio master. If this is satisfactory, then a final answer print is created, from which any subsequent screening prints are struck.

Prints can also be made directly from a video format. Depending on the resolution of the video master, this can be a straightforward method of creating a 35mm print, as no opticals need to be created; titles and effects can all be transferred directly from the video master. This video to film procedure is, however, extremely expensive.

BUDGET SAVING

Although film is an expensive medium, there are a number of ways in which you can reduce the potential costs involved. The costs of shooting on film break down into three main areas: buying stock, hiring camera equipment and processing.

When purchasing stock, it is possible to get substantial discounts. Distributors are competitive in their pricing so you should try as many as possible, and explain the nature of your production. Short ends and re-cans can also be purchased. Short ends are lengths of unexposed stock that have been left over from another shoot, while re-cans are entire rolls of stock that have been loaded into a magazine but never used, so resealed back in the tin. These can be obtained very cheaply and are perfectly fine to shoot a short film on. They should, however, be clip tested to make sure the stock is still good. Clip testing is when a small length of the film is processed to ensure it is performing properly.

There is a huge amount of film camera equipment available for hire. While large rental companies will offer you the latest, most expensive model of a camera, it is also possible to find small companies that will rent older gear that will be perfectly suited to shooting short films on and at fraction of the cost. Always check that any camera you use has been recently tested and is compatible with the rest of your equipment.

Post-production houses and processing labs also run competitive pricing policies, and will often have rates for short films or student films. Because processing and transfer prices are charged by the foot, small fluctuations can make a huge difference when you are processing or transferring thousands of feet. The other way in which you can save money is to provide your own tape stock. When transferring film to video formats, you will also be charged the price of the tape or tapes, and this will generally be much more expensive than if you purchased them yourself. So the cheapest option is to buy them yourself and give them to the lab when you are handing in your rushes.

FILM RESOLUTION

Film negative, though not initially composed of lines, is often transferred into a digital video format for post-production. One of the areas where you can see how far images captured on film out-perform digital capture is with new Digital Intermediate technology, where film negative is scanned into digital files. These files again have a resolution consisting of lines. Currently Super 16mm is scanned at 2K (about 2,000 lines depending on aspect ratio) and 35mm at 4K (about 4,000 lines depending on aspect ratio). 35mm negatives, however, contain so much initial resolution that they can be resolved up to 9K. This amount of information cannot at present be processed at the speeds necessary, but goes some way to showing how much higher-quality film images potentially are, compared to current state of the art digital capture such as HD.

14. SUPER 16MM (S16)

Super 16mm is a film format that is widely used throughout the film and television industry for low-budget feature films, TV dramas, commercials and music promos. It is a very high-resolution format that is ideal for shooting short films that have the necessary budget.

If you are after a cinematic look then S16 is probably the format for you. Although technically less than half the quality of 35mm and without quite the same shallow depth of field capabilities, when used with expertise it can deliver stunning results. Both Super 16mm and standard 16mm formats used to be synonymous with a grainy look that was not comparable to 35mm, but in recent years the technology involved in creating film stocks has improved dramatically. This has led to massive improvements in the quality of the images you can achieve with Super 16mm and made the format more versatile. When combined with the right post-production, its qualities can be enhanced even further.

Super 16mm is shot on 16mm film, but unlike standard 16mm film, which has perforations on both sides of the film and therefore a squarer frame, Super 16mm only has perforations along one side, allowing the rest of the area to be used for the image, giving it a widescreen aspect ratio of 1.66:1 which makes it perfect for transfer to 35mm film or broadcast on 16:9 widescreen television or for transfer to a 35mm print with its similar aspect ratio of 1.85:1.

SUPER 16MM VERSUS 35MM

Super 16mm doesn't have the same image quality that 35mm does, due mainly to the fact that the image is just under half the size of 35mm; but this has many positive repercussions.

Modern S16 cameras and accessories are generally much more diminutive than their 35mm counterparts, in many cases at least half the size; this means that they are lighter and more manoeuvrable. This makes S16 perfect for handheld camera work and situations where the mobility of the camera is paramount. Nearly everything is downsized compared to 35mm, so you are generally dealing with half the mass of equipment, enabling you to move more quickly between shot set ups and even locations, which is vital when you are on a tight schedule and you need to remain mobile.

The smaller image size of Super 16 also means it requires much smaller quantities of light to achieve a properly exposed image. How much light you will need for a given scene depends on what style of lighting you are trying to create and the scope of the shot, but S16 requires less than 35mm and so has better capabilities in situations where you are limited by the amount of artificial light you can obtain. Yet again this can mean substantially less lighting equipment to hire and move about.

The third and very important factor in choosing S16 is the amount that you can shoot on it. Again due to its smaller frame size, a standard 400ft roll of S16 film will allow you to shoot for longer periods than 35mm. At 24 frames per second (FPS) a 400ft roll of S16 will last roughly 11 minutes, whereas a 400ft roll of 35mm will last about 4.5 minutes. The results of this are manifold. On a practical level this means that you can shoot continuously for longer periods, which results in less time being lost changing magazines and loading new ones.

However, the really important benefits of this stock to shooting ratio become apparent when you look at the entire workflow of shooting on film. Not only do you need less stock in the first place, but you also need less processing, transfer, printing and storage capacity.

This is often the reason people choose to shoot on S16 rather than 35mm. Generally most processes, whether it is negative development, telecine or digital scanning, are worked out as a price per foot of your negative. So, for example, if you were having 60 minutes of rushes that you had shot at 24 FPS developed and telecined onto another format, you would be paying an agreed price for each foot of the original negative to go through each process. An hour of rushes on 35mm would be approximately 900ft; on S16 it would only be 364ft.

When you start to look at the financial ramifications of this, then S16 becomes a very cost-efficient format compared to 35mm. As an example for budget comparison, let's imagine that you were going to shoot an hour's worth of rushes on either 35mm or S16mm, then have the negative developed and transferred to a digital format. To achieve this on 35mm you would need roughly 14 x 400ft rolls to shoot for an hour. (35mm colour stock can be anything from 10% to 90% more expensive per roll than S16, but generally about 70% more.) An hour of rushes would be roughly 5,400ft of 35mm negative. On S16 you would need roughly 6 x 400ft rolls of film. An hour of rushes would be roughly 2,160ft.

When you begin to work out the costs entailed you will begin to see how shooting on S16 compared to 35mm can cut costs by dramatic amounts. Obviously it is not always as straightforward as this and can depend on what workflow you are intending to use. If you wanted to have a 35mm screening print at the end of your workflow then there are the costs of getting an optical blow up from S16mm to take into consideration. But as far as shooting and developing are concerned S16 can work out at as much as three times less expensive than 35mm (see format price scale).

For post-production, however, the size of S16 is a drawback. S16 positive prints cannot be screened in cinemas. Because the widescreen aspect ratio uses up the section of the film where conventionally the sound strip would have been, either an expensive 35mm blow up needs to be performed or it has to be transferred to video involving a loss of quality.

SUPER 16MM VERSUS VIDEO

The resolution and performance of S16 is way above standard-definition video. However, high-definition video is only a tiny bit under the resolution of S16 transferred to digital, with many S16 workflows being transferred to HD for post-production and screening. So as far as detail of the image goes, HD is certainly a close rival of S16. However, this is just resolution, and what makes film look like film is the latitude of the colours it can reproduce and the way in which it records the image, allowing for creative use of features such as shallow depth of field, variety of lens types and variable frame rates. There are HD cameras that can reproduce nearly everything that can be achieved with S16, but at present these are the very high-end HD cameras, that may be more expensive to rent for a day than hiring a S16 kit, buying stock and processing.

POTENTIAL WORKFLOWS

Once you have shot your film on S16 there are various different ways that you can work with the rushes to produce a finished film. Due to the fact that S16 is a very high-resolution format, the workflows are designed to preserve its quality. These are examples of common workflows that filmmakers use when having shot on Super 16.

Workflow 1

Shoot on S16 – develop negative – telecine to DV – offline edit – neg cut from EDL – 35mm blow up from 16mm negative.

This workflow may seem complicated but it is actually fairly straightforward. The film stock that has been shot is taken to a lab where the negative is developed. This developed neg is then transferred to video via telecine. The quality and format is not of primary importance here, as this video version is only for offline editing. So for example it could be transferred to MiniDV that could then be loaded onto a computer-based editing system like Final Cut Pro. The footage is then synced with the audio on the computer and edited until a definitive version is finalised. An edit decision list or EDL is then produced from the editing software and given to a neg cutter at the lab who uses it to recreate the computer edit with the original negative. This is then optically blown up to a 35mm print to which a master of the audio can be added thus creating a screening print for exhibition. This is an expensive but very high-quality workflow.

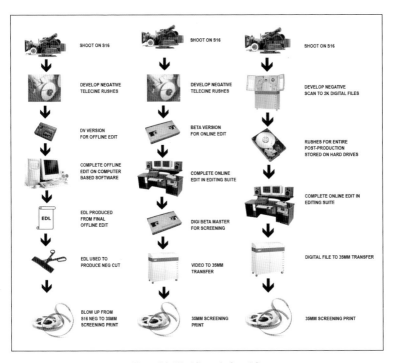

Figure 30. Workflows 1, 2 and 3.

Workflow 2

Shoot on S16 – develop negative – telecine to Digibeta master – online edit – 35mm transfer from Digibeta.

This workflow involves a neg development then telecine transfer to Digibeta. Another version on MiniDV could also be produced for an offline edit. The on-line edit could be performed on an Avid suite with the Digibeta until the final version was reached. This would provide a Digibeta version for screening and could also be transferred to 35mm for exhibition screening.

This is a much more economical workflow, but much of the quality of the original negative is lost in the final version.

Workflow 3

Shoot on S16 – develop negative – digital scan to hard drive at 2K – online edit – 35mm transfer from digital version.

This workflow uses Digital Intermediate Technology. It's very efficient and less expensive than workflow 1, but relies on using a high-end editing system than can handle the large files involved in playing back and manipulating the uncompressed footage. S16 is digitally scanned at a resolution of 2,000 lines (2K), which produces very large digital files.

15. 35MM

35mm film is the industry standard format for shooting and screening feature films. It has been used for filmmaking for over 100 years and, although it has been through many incarnations, still remains unsurpassed in its resolution and general performance.

Despite there being much talk about HD video formats beginning to rival the quality of 35mm film, they are still nowhere near the quality that 35mm provides and the recent improvements in film stock technology have ensured that it will remain the highest resolution format for a very long time.

Everyone will be familiar with the look of 35mm; nearly every major feature film has been shot on it, and in the right hands it has huge capabilities. The colour reproduction and shallow depth of field make it ideal for capturing any type of look.

The only major drawback to shooting your film on 35mm is that it is extremely expensive. This does not just mean that the film stock itself is expensive, but also the cameras, lenses and grip gear that go with it. A larger format than S16, 35mm also requires more light to achieve an adequate exposure. 35mm does not really lend itself to any projects that require small crews and fast working speeds. Choosing 35mm as an acquisition format not only means that you have to have the financial resources, but also the time and patience to create the right conditions for its use.

Academy

35mm is called 35mm because that's how wide the frame is; the film has sprocket holes (perforations) along the edge. The conventional aspect ratio to

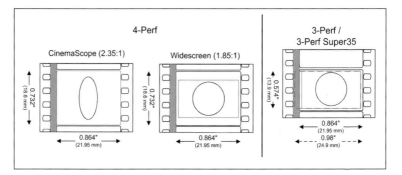

Figure 31. Academy and 3-perf aspect ratios. Image courtesy of www.wikipedia.org.

shoot 35mm at is 1.37:1, which is referred to as academy. This means that each frame has four perforations down its sides. It is, however, not always screened at this aspect ratio. Often it will be letterboxed (see aspect ratio) to give a 1.85:1 widescreen aspect ratio.

3-perf

Because the academy aspect ratio uses the full four perforations of each frame, the resulting image is much larger than is needed, if it is only going to be projected or screened at a 1.85:1 widescreen ratio. This results in there being a lot of waste film that is never shown. 3-perf is a camera system that only pulls down three perforations to create each frame with, which results in an aspect ratio that is instantly closer to 1.85:1 which means less stock is used. The effect of this means a 400ft roll of film will last considerably longer than at normal 4-perf, meaning that processing costs also come down. The only problem with 3-perf is that it cannot be projected, so it is only viable for films undergoing a Digital Intermediate process.

POTENTIAL WORKFLOWS

Film is now usually transferred into a digital form for post-production. Conventionally, 35mm film was edited from an offline edit and then the negative was

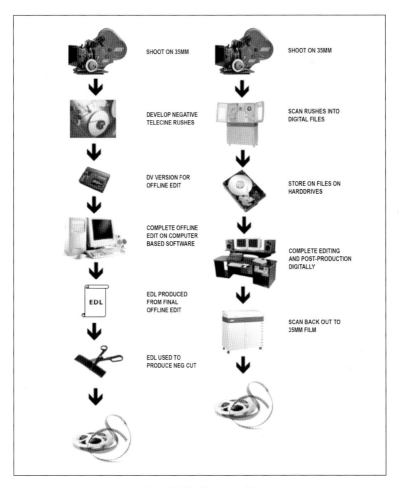

Figure 32. Workflows 1 and 2.

cut from the EDL and prints for screening were made. This is rapidly becoming an obsolete process, however, with more and more 35mm films benefiting from an entirely digital post-production before being laser-scanned back out to a 35mm print. With the advent of cinemas switching to digital projection, the 35mm film screening print will potentially become redundant.

These are examples of common workflows that filmmakers use when shooting on 35mm.

Workflow 1

Shoot on 35mm – develop negative – telecine to DV – offline edit – neg cut from EDL – create positive screening prints.

This is a very traditional workflow for 35mm. Creating an offline DV version allows the film to be digitally edited on a computer, with no need to touch the negative until the final version is ready. A neg cutter then assembles the negative according to the EDL and prints can be made for screening directly from the negative. The drawback to this workflow is that any titles, credits and digital effects need to be created for the 35mm screening prints too, which can be expensive processes.

Workflow 2

Shoot on 35mm – develop negative – digital scan to hard drives at 4K – laser scan to 35mm screening print.

This is a very efficient workflow. The film, once scanned to hard drives, can be edited online and any digital effects, titles or credits can all be added digitally. It can then be scanned back out to a 35mm print.

This is a very expensive workflow and will rely entirely on using professional post-production facilities. This is way beyond the budgets of most short films.

16. LENSES AND FILTERS

The type of lenses with which you choose to make your film has a direct effect on the quality of the image you will be able to record. The higher the quality of the lenses, the clearer and sharper the image you will be recording.

One of the major factors in films' quality and style is the lenses designed for and used with the cameras. However, extremely high-quality cine lenses are no longer just available to people shooting on 16mm or 35mm. High-end video cameras have for some time come with the possibility of interchangeable lenses that allow the user to potentially attach a range of lenses, which means that many of the classic film techniques that require specific lenses can now be achieved on video.

LENS BASICS

Different types of lenses serve different purposes and attaching a different size or type of lens to a film or video camera will give you a different sized image. So, for example, if you set up a camera ten metres from a subject, you could attach different sized lenses, allowing you to create close ups or wide shots without ever moving the camera from its fixed position. This is an important principle to remember. Moving a camera from where it is set up is potentially time-consuming, but by using prime lenses or a zoom lens you can obtain a variety of different types of shot from the same camera position, saving valuable hours and creating a more dynamic variety of shots.

Lenses also change the characteristics of the image, for example wide lenses can give an extreme or subtle curvature to an image also referred to as barrelling, while long lenses can make an image appear flatter. Not simply a byproduct of certain types of lens, this distortion can be used creatively when both choosing a lens for a particular shot and also when cutting between shots created with different lenses during editing.

Lenses function by combining various curved glass elements that can be moved in increments to achieve a sharp, focused image. They also contain an iris that can be adjusted to different sizes or apertures to control the amount of light that passes through it.

LENS TYPES

Focal length

Lenses come in different focal lengths and these focal lengths are referred to in millimetres, so for example 18mm, 50mm, 75mm etc. Each focal length produces a different size of image and perspective.

Different formats require specific ranges of focal lengths, for example a 35mm film camera requires a range of focal lengths designed especially for it. While video formats will have a much smaller image size often recording on to CCD chips seven times smaller than a 35mm film image, so they will have a range of focal lengths based on that.

Even though focal lengths of lenses vary enormously between formats due to image size, the type of image they produce can still be compared, so for example looking through a 35mm film camera with a 50mm lens attached will give you a very similar image as looking through a video camera with a 5.5mm lens attached.

Normal lenses

If you imagine that the focal lengths of any format range from short to long and give you a variety of perspectives, then the mid focal range is what is called normal perspective, because it is the most similar to the perspective of the human eye and so produces a realistic image. Medium focal range lenses give little distortion and are therefore a general-purpose lens for any scenario.

Normal lenses will normally be of these focal lengths, according to format:

- 35mm film: 50mm lens
- S16 film: 25mm lens
- DV: 5.5mm

Wide-angle lenses

Wide-angle lenses are lenses with shorter focal lengths. They provide a more extreme perspective, creating a wider frame by pushing the perspective further back than where the camera itself is actually placed. They are frequently used for creating an impression of greater space and the distortion they produce can make actors or props appear larger than they actually are. Extreme wide-angle lenses or fish-eye lenses will produce a very noticeable distortion that is often used for visual effect.

Wide-angle lenses will normally be of these focal lengths, according to format:

- 35mm film: 9.5 downwards
- S16 film: 6.5 downwards
- DV: 3.4 downwards

Telephoto lenses

Telephoto lenses are lenses with longer focal lengths. Long lenses produce a close perspective with a smaller frame that brings you closer to the subject than where the camera is physically placed. Telephoto lenses produce a very flat, tight image and can be used for close ups to shoot subjects from greater distances. The disadvantage of telephoto lenses is that they magnify movement, shake or wobble, while controlling the camera will appear much more severe when using a long lens.

Telephoto lenses will normally be of these focal lengths, according to format:

- 35mm film: 135mm
- S16 film: 50mm
- DV: 20mm

Prime lenses

Prime lenses are lenses with a fixed focal length. These focal lengths are normally combined into sets of lenses that will cover everything that you would conventionally need for filming a scene. Sets of lenses will range from short to long lengths covering intervals in between; by using a combination of prime lenses in a conventional set, it's possible to create a dynamic range of shot perspectives. Although a zoom lens may cover the focal lengths of prime lenses, primes normally produce higher-quality images and are faster, so can be used with less light. Sets of prime lenses will normally consist of these focal lengths according to format:

- 35mm film: 18mm, 25mm, 50mm, 85mm
- S16 film: 9.5mm, 12mm, 16mm, 25mm
- DV: see video lens adapter

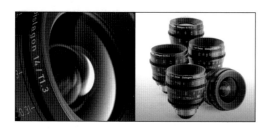

Figure 33.
Set of super speed Zeiss
Prime lenses. Image
courtesy of Arri Group.

Zoom lenses

Unlike prime lenses that are fixed at a particular focal length, zoom lenses allow you to move between ranges of focal lengths and can be used either at a fixed length or by moving between them, to create a zoom shot. Zoom lenses have the obvious advantage that they don't constantly need to be changed. However, due to their nature, they aren't capable of producing the same quality as using prime lenses; they are often slower-speed lenses than primes, so need more light to shoot with.

FOCUS

Whether you are using low or high-quality lenses, it's critical to ensure that the focus is as sharp as you can possibly achieve. Video cameras will often provide an auto focus function, but this is not suitable for the needs of most filmmakers, so manually focusing the camera is the preferred option. This can either be adjusted by eye, or by measuring. Eye focusing is fast, but not very precise. Due to the size of viewfinders, it is often hard to distinguish whether what you are seeing is sharp or not.

Some prosumer video cameras offer a function that will highlight the focused area of the frame with red lines, which can help tell you when things have gone out of focus, but the task of focusing the camera while following the action can still remain difficult.

Measuring the distances is the most precise way of achieving a crisp image. Most professional film lenses are designed to be used in this way. The lenses are marked with calibrated distances at which they will focus. So setting the lens marking to 2.8m means that the focus will be precisely at that distance from the lens. When using higher-resolution formats and professional quality lenses, there is more opportunity to achieve a super-sharp image; although this is an obvious advantage, the downside is that any image that isn't correctly focused will be much more noticeable and appear softer. This is why, on professional shoots, it's standard procedure to measure the distance to the subject and set the lens focus manually. Normally the focus puller attaches a tape measure to the top of the camera and measures off to a point, or range of points if the camera or subject is going to move. These measurements are then marked on the follow focus, so that the lens can be adjusted between them fluidly during the shot, ensuring that the focus is maintained at all times.

Although all professional lenses will be calibrated with focus distances, different focal lengths will only be able to focus within certain ranges. Beyond

Figure 34. Camera assistant measuring off the focus.

these ranges, the lenses will reach an infinity marking which appears as an eight turned on its side; anything beyond this point will be in focus, but not as sharp as within the distance markings.

APERTURE

Exposure is the other critical function of lenses. The amount of exposure is controlled by the degree to which the iris of the lens is opened. The size of this aperture determines how much light is let through. This is calibrated on the lens in numbers that are referred to as stops. On stills camera lenses these are known as F-numbers or stops, but, to differentiate, film lenses are marked with T-stops. The lower the T-stop the wider the iris is open and the more light is let in. The higher the T-stop, the smaller the aperture and the less light is let in. Conventional T-stops will run from a low figure such as T 2.0 to T 22. How low the lowest T-stop figure is depends on the speed of the lens (see lens speed).

Setting the right aperture is imperative to producing a well-exposed image, and is dependent on the speed of stock (when shooting on film) and the amount of light available. This is set either by an 'in camera' light meter, or more accurately with a handheld light meter. The aperture setting has an influence on the lens's ability to focus (see depth of field).

Depth of field (DOF)

Depth of field is one of the most important aspects of lenses and formats. Everyone will be familiar with shots in films where only a certain object will be in focus, or the profile of a face, while the rest of the image remains out of focus. This technique is used widely and creatively throughout filmmaking, and allows the director to draw the audience's attention to particular details and aspects of an image. This is achieved by creating a shallow depth of field.

Depth of field is the distance covered by a lens that will be in focus. If you focus a lens on an object three metres away then there will be a distance either side of that object which will also be in focus. How great or small those distances are will be determined by the aperture setting on the camera. The lower the T-stop the shallower the depth of field becomes. So for instance with a low T-stop aperture setting, focusing on the object three metres away might give a depth of field of ten centimetres either side of the object, but with a high t-stop aperture setting, it may focus a metre either side. Depth of field therefore requires large apertures and is also dependent on the image size of the format. Video formats have a lot of depth of field due to their

 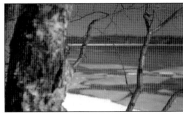

Figure 35. Shots making use of shallow depth of field achieved with the Brevis 35 adapter on HDV format, shot by Denis Wood. www.cinevate.com

small image size, which is why it is difficult (see video adapters) to create the same shallow depth of field that you can achieve with film formats such as S16 and 35mm.

LENS SPEED

The other significant differentiating factor amongst lenses is what's referred to as their speed. The speed of a lens is the amount of light it can let in at its widest aperture. This is a very important consideration when choosing a lens or set of lenses to shoot with. Slower lenses, which will start with a higher T-stop, mean that they can only be used in conditions where there is at least enough light to reach this first stop. Fast speed lenses, often called super-speed lenses, will have a very low first stop, meaning they are ideal for low-light situations.

Figure 36.
Lens aperture T-stops.

Mounts

Different sets of lenses are designed for different formats, but, within those formats, lenses will also have a particular type of mount. Some of these are specific to the make of a type of camera, such as *Aaton mount* or *Panavision mount*, which means those lenses can only be attached to a camera with the same mount. There are also universal mounts, such as *PL* or *PV*, which can be found on different makes of camera and so any lens with the equivalent mount can be used. It is also possible to find adapters for many common lens mounts. When hiring sets of lenses it's important to check that the mounts are compatible with the camera.

Video lens adapters

For a long time, one of the major advantages of shooting on film was the quality and behaviour of the lenses involved. Shallow depth of field and general quality of the lenses contributes hugely to the look of film. Video formats due to their comparatively tiny image size and small CCD chips could not benefit from high-quality lenses and the 'film look'. The first step towards remedying this was the advent of video cameras with interchangeable lenses. However, because of the smaller image size of video, if you simply placed a 35mm film lens on the camera, you would only be using a tiny fraction of the whole lens. This dilemma has recently been solved by the invention of adapters that are designed to enable the use of film lenses with video cameras. They work by projecting the 35mm lens image into a series of prisms that reduce its size to that of the video image. This then means the whole lens is used, and behaves in the same way as if it were on a 35mm camera so you can produce the same shallow depth of field that you can with film. The overall quality that the lenses produce gives amazing quality video images. The adapters are designed to be used with sets of both film and photographic prime lenses.

There are currently several versions on the market:

BREVIS 35
RedRock Micro M2
Mini35 Digital adapter from *P+S Technik*
MOVIEtube ST or *PRO*

MATTE BOX

Matte boxes serve two functions. Their primary function is to cover the peripheries of the lens so that light can't refract into the lens from the sides and ruin exposure settings and image quality. If the matte box isn't enough within itself, then extension pieces known as *French Flags* are attached to it.

The second function of matte boxes is to allow filters to be inserted into removable trays that then cover the lens.

FILTERS

Filters perform a variety of functions that will directly affect the images you are capturing. When shooting on film, filters are commonly used in conjunction with certain types of stock or lighting to rectify possible imbalances. Filters can also be used for purely aesthetic reasons on both film and video, allowing you to create a mood or tone or enhance what is already there. The other types of filters widely used in cinematography are neutral density filters and polarising filters.

Neutral density filters, or NDs, are used to filter the amount of light coming into the lens. They come in varying degrees of transparency and are also used in bright light situations to enable wide apertures for shallow depth of field.

Polarisers filter light as well but they filter reflected light from surfaces, for instance reducing glare from windows or reflective surfaces.

FOLLOW FOCUS

A follow focus is used to accurately and smoothly control focus settings. Focusing a lens by hand while operating a camera can be difficult or impossible to do, and is normally performed with a follow focus device that attaches to the camera and is operated not by the DP but by a camera assistant. Using a combination of wheels and gears, the follow focus allows a focus puller or camera operator to make fluid changes in focus. Generally the focus distances will have been measured before the shot allowing the puller to mark them on the follow focus discs and turn the mechanism smoothly between them.

17. LIGHTING

Whichever format and type of camera you decide to shoot on, it's important to remember that, to fully capitalise on its potential quality, then you need to use it under its optimum conditions. The key factor to creating these conditions is light.

Lighting for either film or video has two major functions, both of which are crucial to creating a quality image.

EXPOSURE

The first is exposure. Whether you are using film or video, you need to create an environment where there is enough light to record a well-exposed image. Both film stock and CCD chips are dependent on receiving an adequate amount of light to produce images. And adequate doesn't just mean enough light for the camera to pick up an image. Although most cameras, especially video, will be able to record an image in low-light conditions, the quality of that image is going to be very poor. The camera will potentially be able to compensate for the lack of available light by digitally enhancing the image within the camera, but the resulting image is going to be pixelated and lack definition. Similarly with film cameras, using a high-speed film may allow you to film in very poorly lit environments, but unless there is enough light to expose things properly, then again the image quality will suffer and you will end up with a grainy image with no distinct detail.

So when planning your shoot you should ensure that there are high enough light levels for whichever format or camera you are going to use. Natural light may need to be boosted with artificial film lighting and even practical lights, such as domestic lamps, may need to be fitted with brighter photo bulbs until you have raised the light levels to a satisfactory level.

MOOD

To merely light for your film practically in order to achieve adequate light levels would be to miss out on one of the major creative elements in filmmaking.

Lighting has the potential to bring your film to life. Just as you would try and get an actor to deliver a line of script in a certain tone or mood, so too should you try and match your lighting to the tone and mood of your film's narrative. Not only will lighting enhance a line of script or an actor's expression, it will give the entire film a unified feel.

DP

If you are using an experienced DP, then it is important that you discuss the style and feel of the lighting you want for individual scenes and the film as a whole. If you don't have the terminology to describe what you want, then your best resource is using examples from other films or photographs.

Large-scale lighting set ups are time-consuming and labour-intensive to create. Always discuss with your DP or lighting designer as early as possible the budget that you have for lighting (including gaffers and sparks) as well as the amount of time you will have at various locations. Both you and the DP will need to work within the limitations of your budget to achieve the look you want. Changing a location or altering a scene could both be legitimate compromises that might need to be made if lighting for your original idea is not a possibility.

LIGHTING YOURSELF

Lighting for film is an art form in its own right and achieving simple set ups can be incredibly difficult and time-consuming. If you aren't working with a DP and are planning on lighting your own film, then to achieve the look and feel you want it is important to practice. With a basic lighting kit of three lights with stands you can, given enough time and practice, achieve very sophisticated results.

Perfecting different lighting set ups prior to your shoot, when time is not at a premium, will pay dividends when it comes to the look of your finished film. The important thing to remember when lighting yourself is to be as methodical as possible; rushing your lighting or employing a haphazard approach will produce uneven and awkward results.

Light = Danger

Film lighting is extremely dangerous. Whether it's a single redhead or a studio full of 10K lights, the potential hazard is high. Film lights, their casings and anything on which they are focused for long enough will get extremely hot. Hot enough to cook or melt plastic and set combustible materials on fire. Regardless of whether you are shooting in a studio with stringent health and safety guidelines or at a friend's flat with no guidelines, you should always take the utmost care in making sure you are not endangering yourself or anyone else in the cast and crew. Always double check that you, your gaffer or whichever crew member is responsible for placing lighting is following these basic rules.

- Never touch any lighting even momentarily without wearing heatproof gloves.
- Check that lights are securely fastened to stands or attachments.
- Make sure the stands are adequately held in place with sand bags or fastenings and there is no chance of them tipping over, even when pulled or knocked.
- Ensure that all cables are securely fastened to any floor area they are trailing over. Generously gaffer-taping them down is the normal practice.
- Do not have any bottles of water, cups of tea, soft drinks or other fluids within the immediate vicinity of lights or generators.
- Make it very clear to the rest of the cast and crew before you turn the lights on just how potentially hazardous they can be. Keep anyone who doesn't need to be in close proximity to the lighting as far away as possible.

- If a light can't be securely placed, or is precariously placed, don't use it. You are trying to make a film, not a disaster!

LIGHT TEMPERATURE AND COLOUR

All light sources, whether natural or artificial, have a temperature; this temperature affects the colour of the light. Light temperature is measured in Kelvin, with lower-temperature light sources having a much warmer colour and higher-temperature light sources having a much colder colour. So for example, the extremely high-temperature light source that the sun provides gives a cold blue light, while a candle or domestic light are much lower temperatures and produce a warmer orange light. Although the human eye is extremely sensitive, it often cannot perceive the extreme colour contrast that exists between light sources. Yet they are often very apparent when captured on film stock or video, and the difference between artificial light and daylight is often a major factor in determining how a scene has to be lit and light sources matched according to their colour.

White balance/colour balance

White balance is really a video term used to describe colour balance. Because different types of light produce different hues of colour, images produced in certain light conditions whether on video or film will be affected by the colour of the light. This can often be rectified by either correcting or replacing the light sources, using special film stocks, or in post-production, using a colour grading process. With many video cameras, however, it is possible to instantly rectify the colour balance in camera. By selecting the purest white within a shot the balance can be adjusted back to a pure white hue. The same principle exists when shooting on film, where a colour chart and neutral grey card are used as corrective references for the processing lab.

BRIGHTNESS

In filmmaking, lights and lighting are generally referred to in watts, so for instance common film lights are just called 800watts or 2,000watts because that's how much power they use and therefore how much light is outputted. Although this only refers to the type of lamp or bulb they use it is also often an indication of the size of the light itself. Regardless of the type or power of the light sources, the amount of light that they produce needs to be monitored and controlled to achieve a well-exposed image.

LIGHT METER

To control the amount of light you use for a scene and achieve an even exposure, you need to be able to measure the amount of light. For this you use a light meter. Light meters allow the DP to precisely measure the amount of light falling onto a subject, or part of a subject, and adjust the light sources until the desired variety of high light and low light tones are produced. The basic principle of light meters is that they allow you to input a shutter speed, so for instance 25 FPS, and then take a light reading. The light meter then gives you a reading in F-stops or T-stops, which correlates with the aperture markings on the lens and allows you to set it accordingly, opening the aperture to let more light in or vice versa.

There are two basic types of light metering: reflected light and incident light. Many cameras have internal reflected light meters that use a sensor to record the overall light reflected from the subject into the lens. Although reflected light meters are useful, because they only give an overall average reading of the whole shot, elements within it could still be over or under exposed. For greater accuracy a handheld incident light meter can be used, which uses a small light-sensitive sphere that can be held directly in front of the subject and directed towards the camera, giving a more precise reading and ensuring that the exposure is set for the subject rather than the overall light in the shot. Spot meters can also be used, a form of reflected light meter that can offer a greater degree of accuracy, allowing you to pinpoint small areas such as a highlight on a forehead, and check for potential overexposure.

Prosumer video cameras now offer an advanced reflective light meter reading, known as zebra function. This highlights potentially under or over exposed areas of the frame by showing diagonal lines. Similar to a spot meter, even tiny areas of the frame can be pinpointed for greater accuracy.

TYPES OF LIGHT

Film and video lights

For precision lighting, ranges of professional film lights are needed. Depending on the scale and scope of lighting required for your film, a lighting kit can consist of anything from three basic lights that you can place on stands and plug into a domestic power supply, to several lorry loads of lighting that will require generators, scaffolding rigs and a crew of gaffers and sparks to set them up and adjust them.

Tungsten

The most common type of film lighting that you will come across for film-making is tungsten-based lighting. These lights are so called because they have a tungsten filament that provides a bright, even source with a steady colour temperature. They are the industry standard, and film stocks and video cameras are specifically designed to be used with them. Standard tungsten lights come in various wattages, starting at about 400w and ranging up to 12,000w. The commonest lighting set ups for short films on a small budget are often produced with kits of three 800w lights, known as redheads, and 2,000w lights known as blondes.

Regardless of the wattage, there are two main types of tungsten light, either open face or Fresnel. Open face lights produce an evenly distributed light source, but Fresnel use a glass optic which allows you to focus the light, so that you can produce a wide or floodlit source or a narrow or spotlit source.

Fluorescent

Domestic fluorescent lights can't really be used for film lighting due to their flicker and colour temperature. There are a variety of professional film lights that work using tungsten-balanced fluorescent bulbs, often in groups to create banks of lighting. The two advantages of these lights are that they instantly provide a soft, diffused lighting source and that they do not generate the type of extreme heats that you get with other film lighting. This makes them ideal for using in small, enclosed locations, as they can be used to directly light sources and, due to their cool temperature, placed close to the subject.

HMI

HMI lights are a type of Arc lighting, which create a light source by burning an arc of gas between two points. They are capable of burning extremely brightly and are often used for creating artificial daylight. This is a specialist light even within professional filmmaking and is only required for certain circumstances that require very powerful light sources. You are much more likely to be using tungsten lights on a short film.

Practical lights

If you are on a small budget, then one of the most effective strategies for lighting your film, that doesn't involve hiring large amounts of lighting, generators, gaffers and sparks, is to use what is already there. If you are shooting a domestic interior, then you have the possibility of using the existing lighting sources. Domestic lights such as ceiling light fixtures or table lamps etc are referred to as 'practical lights'. It is not often the case that standard domestic bulbs will have a high enough wattage to create enough exposure for the camera, so these bulbs can be replaced with high-wattage photo bulbs, which are comparatively cheap and easy to obtain from photographic shops. Using combinations of practical lighting such as table lamps is a convenient way to effectively create mood lighting for your film. If you are planning on using practical lighting sources with photo bulbs then care and precautions should be taken. Photo bulbs are much brighter and therefore much hotter than standard domestic bulbs; the amount of heat they generate can easily set fire to, or heat to scorching temperatures, anything in close proximity to them.

Work lights

Due to the very high costs of either purchasing or hiring film lighting, many independent and short filmmakers have looked for alternatives. Tungsten work lights are often a viable alternative to professional lighting, available from hardware stores at a tiny fraction of the cost of professional film lights; they can even have barn doors made for them. The disadvantage of the low cost is that they are less easy to control and tend to hotspot (create an uneven throw of light).

THE CHEAPEST LIGHT

For short filmmakers, using what is available is the key to creating a good-looking film on a small budget. Often the cheapest and most practical source of lighting is natural daylight. As with film lights, it is possible to control daylight; using a combination of diffusion and reflection techniques, you can easily achieve stunning natural daylight shots on the smallest of budgets. Although there is no hire charge or electricity bill to pay with natural daylight, it does have its limits. The winter months give extremely short shooting periods, while the summer months produce long but very bright conditions, making spring and autumn the most suitable times for shooting outside.

LIGHT CONTROL

When lighting for a shot or a scene, you are essentially trying to enhance the shape and form of what you are going to film. To achieve the control needed for accurate and skilful lighting, there are a number of variables that allow the source and quality of light to be manipulated, namely intensity, size, shape and colour.

Diffusion

Tungsten lights are hardly ever used directly pointing at a subject; this type of lighting creates very harsh contrasts, producing deep shadows. Occasionally a desired look, it is generally seen as an attractive lighting style in filmmaking. To avoid this, diffusion is used to change the intensity of a light source by softening it. This creates a gentler feel by spreading the light and softening the harsh edges of shadows. Diffusers come in many different forms. Certain fabrics such as silk are used to create screens or soft boxes, where frames are covered in diffusing fabric, allowing for a soft, even light source.

Trace (also known as diffuser) is also commonly used for this purpose, similar in consistency to tracing paper. It comes in various densities, and is designed to withstand the heat of the lights. An appropriately sized section is removed from the roll and can either be attached directly to the barn doors of the light, or to a frame that the light passes through. Trace is normally calibrated to the stops of a light meter, so that various densities or layers can be used to reduce the intensity of a light by half-a-stop increments. Trace can also be used to control daylight sources, attaching sections to window frames or sticking it directly on to the panes.

Scrims are wire meshes of different densities that you attach to the front of the light. Because lighting comes in a series of fixed wattages, you choose brightness close to what you need and then use scrims to reduce the intensity of the light beam. They are calibrated to the same lighting ranges as light meters, so that a placing a single scrim on a light will reduce its brightness by half a stop.

Bouncing a light source is often the easiest way to instantly create a diffused light source. The simplest method is often to bounce the light beam off an existing surface such as the ceiling or a wall, but when this is not possible, reflectors can be used. Pieces of white polystyrene board are commonly used to bounce light back into a scene as well as screens of silver or gold fabric, allowing the direction of the reflected light to be precisely controlled. Huge frames with large silks attached can also be used to diffuse daylight when shooting outdoors. The most desirable option is often to shoot on a day with even cloud cover, where the clouds create diffusion and produce a natural soft light.

Shape

Barn doors

Barn doors are metal shutters that are attached to the front of a light. They normally consist of four folding metal flaps that can be configured to create different shaped beams. This allows you to create everything from a narrow slit, to a wide-open beam. For more precise shapes of light, snoots are used. These are funnel shapes that can be attached to the front of the light and are used to create certain shapes, such as round pools or rectangular forms.

Flags

Flags are used to block areas of a beam of light, often attached to lighting stands. They normally consist of a metal frame that is covered with fabric, either a scrim material to reduce the amount of light, or a black material to completely block the light.

Colour

Gels

Gels are used to control the colour of the light source. They are available in a spectrum of different colours, and usually available on rolls. The appropriately sized piece is removed from the roll and can be attached to the barn doors of a light, frame or window. Different coloured gels can be used to create mood or compensate for discrepancies in the type of temperature light you are using. For example, using a combination of daylight and artificial light which have different colour temperatures, it is possible to match them, either using gels on the tungsten lights, or gels on the windows; these are known as colour balancing gels or corrective gels.

THE BASICS OF LIGHTING A SCENE

Different locations, moods and circumstances all call for individually crafted lighting set ups, but the basic principles for lighting a scene or individual subject are often based around the three point lighting technique. Although it won't provide you with a principle for every lighting situation, it can be used as a basis to create very sophisticated lighting effects from. The beauty of three point lighting technique is its versatility. You can create it with three 800w redheads in a tiny environment, or thirty 12,000w in a huge environment; the type and power of the lighting involved makes no difference to the principle, just the scale you can use it on.

Key light

When beginning to light a new scene the best thing is to start methodically with all the lights turned off and the subject in the general position they will adopt for that shot or scene. The first step is to establish from which direction your most prominent source of light should be coming from, which is generally slightly in front of and above the subject, adjusting angle and height accordingly. This is termed the key light and is the first light you should turn on and position. This doesn't have to be just one light, it could be several, depending on how much light is needed. A variety of diffusion methods can also be used to create the quality of light you want to obtain.

Once you have successfully positioned the key light, the subject will be lit only from one angle, illuminating anything in its path, but also creating dark shadows.

Fill light

The principle of the fill light is to counteract and reduce the shadows produced by the key, giving the subject more form. The fill light is generally placed at the opposite angle and side of the subject to the key light.

Again, a fill light does not have to be one single light source; a variety of smaller light sources can be used in various positions. As a general rule the fill light should start off being about half as bright as the key light, but can be adjusted accordingly.

Backlight

Once the key and fill lights are in place, you move on to the last in the trilogy, the backlight. People often think that the backlight illuminates the background scenery. This is not the function of the backlight, but an additional light often referred to as a kicker, which is really another type of fill light, often used to remove shadows created by the key.

The backlight is placed behind the subject and angled directly towards it. The purpose of the backlight is to give the subject an illuminated edge, literally a rim of light which makes them stand out from the background, which is why the backlight is also often referred to as the rim light.

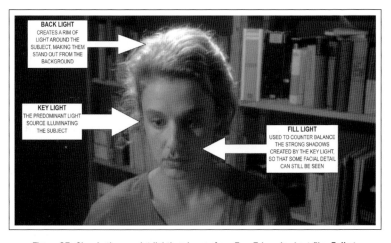

Figure 37. Classic three point lighting. Image from Tom Tykwer's short film *Epilog*.

18. GRIP GEAR

TRIPOD

Unless you are shooting entirely handheld then you are going to need a tripod or tripods. It's easy to think of the tripod as just something to hold the camera up, but a good tripod will do more than simply stabilise your camera and can make a huge difference to the look of your film, whatever format you are making it on. While cheaper domestic models may suffice for lightweight video cameras, they will be limited in what can be achieved with them. Professional tripods, however, will allow you to create well-executed camera moves such as panning and tilting. Most pro tripods will come in two parts.

Fluid head

Fluid heads allow you to create smooth combinations of panning and tilting movements rather than just one or the other; variables such as resistance and direction can be precisely controlled to produce fluid moves at different speeds.

Legs

Pro tripods will have a bowl of a specific size into which the head is inserted. As long as the bowl size matches that of the head then you can use various lengths and weights of legs. When hiring a tripod for a shoot, you often take two sets of legs, tall and short, as well as a high hat for ultra-low shots.

The size and weight you will need depends on the nature and format of your shoot; they are also referred to as sticks.

TRACK AND DOLLY

To create tracking shots you need lengths of track and a dolly to go on it. Professional dollies are extremely heavy and run on modular lengths of straight or curved metal track or can have pneumatic tyres put on them and run on the ground. They provide a range of features, from pneumatic jibbing to extra seating for use without track.

Lightweight doorway dollies come in all shapes and sizes; they are ideal for lightweight formats and quick to set up. The quality of the shots you can achieve with them is significantly less than with a heavyweight version, but they are still extremely effective. You can even make a homemade version from skateboard wheels that run on lengths of drainpipe. Wheelchairs are often used, with the cameraman being pushed around to achieve a similar, if slightly less controlled, effect.

Figure 38.
Chapman Super PeeWee III dolly.

JIB/BOOM

A jib is a small boom arm that can be connected to a tripod or dolly. The camera is attached to one end and then counterbalanced at the other with a set of weights. The jib can then perform a seesaw motion, producing smooth swooping camera moves. Professional jibs are serious pieces of equipment that really need a qualified grip to operate them; however, there are also smaller lightweight jibs designed for the DV market that are easy to use and produce fairly impressive results.

Figure 39.
Cambo Lightweight
Jibbing boom arm with
video camera.

STEADICAM

Steadicam, unlike most other grip gear, allows the camera to be moved smoothly on multiple axes at the same time. By combining a counterbalance for the camera with a mechanised arm attached to a support vest, the operator can walk or run, while simultaneously panning and tilting.

Figure 40.
Tiffen Steadicam in action,
operated by Nick Bennett.

The potential steadicam gives for sophisticated camera moves is unparalleled; however, rehearsing and perfecting these moves takes time and will complicate what potentially might be a straightforward shot.

Steadicam is a registered product that is expensive to hire and needs to be operated by a professional. However, much cheaper, less versatile versions are available for lightweight DV camera work, although using them skilfully still requires a fair amount of experience.

19. HIRING EQUIPMENT

Whether you need a camera, lighting or microphone, the chances are that some element in creating your short film will involve you hiring equipment, probably from a professional hire company. There are two main types of hire that most companies offer: dry hire and wet hire.

WET HIRE

Wet hire is hiring equipment that comes with either an operator or supervisor. This is a less common type of hire, but necessary if the piece of equipment requires a specialist or certified operator. When hiring any piece of kit the rental house will always expect the people hiring to be able to use the equipment safely and proficiently; with cameras and sophisticated equipment the rental company will often require a demonstration by the hirers to prove that they know the equipment well enough to use it. If you require an item that you or someone in your team doesn't know how to use, then most rental houses will offer the option of wet hire, or a training day for the hirer to get accustomed to specific pieces of kit.

DRY HIRE

Dry hire is the most common type of film equipment hire, where equipment can be booked and then picked up before the shoot. However well you or a member of your crew knows a piece of equipment, it is always important that you leave enough time to check each individual item that you are hiring; whether it is a lens or a whole camera, time needs to be taken to check that it is functioning properly. This is vital, as not only will a faulty piece of equipment jeopardise your film, but also leave you liable to take the responsibility when it is returned. Rigorously checking each item avoids both such situations.

BUDGET SAVING

Filmmaking technology is constantly evolving, and the consequences for short filmmakers are twofold. Not only can you get sophisticated gear with which to make your film, it also means that there is a huge amount of filmmaking equipment not really in use.

Equipment rental companies, post-production facilities and so on are required to keep up to date with new technologies because big budget productions want to use them. This process of constant updating means equipment that was state of the art a decade ago might now be nearly obsolete. Just because it's no longer at the cutting edge doesn't mean it isn't still high-quality or professional. When hiring gear or booking facilities, don't get the latest, newest equipment they have but opt for the equipment they use less frequently and as back up.

It will have been well-maintained and be perfectly usable for the purposes of your short. Just because the kit isn't cutting edge, doesn't mean your film won't be. This approach will potentially save you a small fortune and you will be much more likely to get cheap rates or substantial discounts. You should also get much more kit, which will potentially make your film technically more professional.

When dealing with any professional filmmaking company, whether you're hiring a costume, prop or camera, you mustn't expect to get something for nothing. It may seem logical that they would give your small-budget film everything for a proportional amount but post-production facilities, and especially rental houses, have to keep their equipment maintained to the highest standards. Every time a camera or light goes out, or an editing suite is used, it requires time and effort to check and prepare it for the next rental, all of which can be a labour-intensive process. Luckily, most people that run these companies tend to be passionate about filmmaking, and may well want to help you out, but you will need to bear the following in mind.

The best strategy is to try and get the most you can for what you have. Don't call and ask for everything for free. Try and offer as much as you can afford, however little that may be. Work around them. All film companies will have down time, periods when they will have low workloads or quiet spells, so ask them to let you know when these occur. Even then don't ask for the newest, most expensive gear, because they will inevitably need it back the soonest. Explain your project to them. Try and get them as enthused about what you are doing as you are. Explain that it is a non-profit endeavour and you would appreciate anything they could offer, even if it's not everything you need for the project. Film industry employees will be extremely knowledge-able and potentially helpful, so even if you don't get the deal you're after, you may well walk away with some useful information for your project. Always offer film credits to anyone who offers you a deal or help of any nature; it's the least you can do.

Sadly, there is not really such a thing as a free piece of professional film equipment; nearly anything that you are offered will need to be insured and the more expensive the value of the kit, the higher the insurance costs will be.

20. DIRECTING

Being the director of a film entails much more than just directing a shoot. On short films especially, the director will be deeply involved in every step of the entire production and guide the project through all of the stages to its completion. Directing the shoot, however, requires the director to develop a set of practical skills and considerations that will help control the way in which the material is brought to life.

WORKING WITH ACTORS

Acting is really an act of translation, in which the actor interprets the script and portrays the actions and emotions of the material to an audience. A good performance relies on both the talent of the actor to convey these elements convincingly and the skill of the director in eliciting a good performance. It's possible to have a natural, raw talent for both, but each improves with practice and requires the source material to have potential in the first place.

Directing actors can be a difficult or effortless undertaking. The key to producing a good performance really lies in your ability to cast the right actor. If you have succeeded in this then you should be able to guide the actor through the script, helping them to draw out the emotional content of the material you want to emphasise. The best approach to working with actors is simply to communicate with them as naturally and clearly as you can. You also need to give the actors as much opportunity as possible to give a good performance and understand the nature of what they are performing. Ensuring that actors have adequate time to learn scripts and develop a performance, by holding read-through sessions and rehearsals, should enable both you and the actors to get a better grasp of the material and improve performances.

Expecting actors to produce pitch-perfect performances on a single take is extremely unrealistic. If you are shooting minimal shooting ratios, due to time or stock limitations, then you shouldn't expect your cast to necessarily meet those imposed limits. Capturing a good performance takes time and patience.

Body language

As a director you are working with combinations of two major elements, body language and delivery. Body language is probably the more difficult of the two elements to direct. Roles that require little or no dialogue are often much more strenuous for an actor than those with; portraying complex emotions while limited to facial expressions and gestures is very demanding. Even with roles that require dialogue, the subtleties that body language conveys are often more important than the dialogue. As director you should consider and monitor body language constantly, trying out different subtle variations until you find the right combination.

Delivery

The way in which dialogue is delivered should be one of your primary concerns. How convincing a single line or phrase will sound relies on the intonation and emotion of one actor. For conversational dialogue, you also need to consider the timing involved between several people. Directing delivery requires you to help the actors develop the pace and rhythm. Read-throughs prior to the shoot should allow you and the actors to become familiar with the material and evolve a natural rhythm. This can then be fine-tuned by potentially pin-pointing certain phrases or even words that you think require more or less emphasis, while ensuring that the overall pace and timing is coherent.

Sometimes dialogue that reads well on a page simply doesn't sound convincing when spoken, so never be afraid to change a line or even a whole page of script if it is not working. Good delivery doesn't just rely on the talent of the actor interpreting it, but also on the quality of the script.

Motivation

Motivation is the most essential direction that you can give to an actor. Although it may seem obvious to you (as a scriptwriter perhaps), the emotions that a character is supposed to be feeling at any moment may not necessarily be clear to the actor; and the non-chronological way in which you shoot a film also means that you may be moving quickly between scenes that require very different dramatic tones. It is therefore important to pinpoint the dramatic needs of the characters and work with the actor on generating their consequent body language and delivery.

Blocking

Blocking is the process of working out your actors' placement and movement for a shot or whole scene. This takes careful consideration: you need to consider not just the dramatic needs of the scene but also the position of the camera and lighting. In a sense the actors need to serve the camera and lighting, rather than the other way round, so that you can keep those elements as fixed as possible. Realistically, under the pressure of time, it is much quicker and easier to manoeuvre an actor than it is to relight a scene or shift a camera.

Walk through

When the actors need to perform a movement, whether it's a gesture or moving through a room, the most effective method for getting them to understand what you want is to show them yourself, or walking through it with them.

Walking through a scene with an individual should make it easy to understand what you have in mind as far as direction, business, placement and speed are concerned. This process will also help you to see their viewpoint from within a scene and the DP to find the right lens or move to cover any action.

Hitting marks

If you are directing complicated movements or if focus is critical in a scene, then the easiest way to get the actors to their positions is to put marks on the floor, making sure that they are not in shot. The camera can be pre-focused to these marks during a walk through.

Run through

Once you have blocked out the action for a scene or shot, and maybe done a walk through, you will often need to do a run through. This is for you and the DP to make sure it is possible to capture all the action, and to give the actors a last practice chance. With so many unpredictable things that can occur during a take, it really pays to fine-tune a scene before you roll the camera. However, if you are after a certain kind of spontaneity then you have to be careful not to kill the performances by over-rehearsing.

Mise-en-scene

Mise-en-scene refers to how you put a scene together; it's a broad term for anything that makes up the frame of a shot, so placement of actors, props, lighting and so on.

SHOOTING RATIO

A shooting ratio is the amount of footage you shoot compared to how much goes into the final cut of the film, so shooting 20 minutes for a 10-minute film would be expressed as a 2:1 ratio. Much like a golf par, it consists of how many takes you have to do per shot to get the one you need, and just like golf you need to keep a scorecard.

Every take and its length will be noted by a camera assistant, but it's also important for the director to remain aware of how many takes are being averaged. If you are shooting on film then this is crucial. The amount of stock you have will be limited, and will dictate your shooting ratio; otherwise you are going to run out of film before you've finished the project.

A shooting ratio is an average, so if you do 15 takes for one shot and 3 for another you would average a 9:1 ratio, which means you can quickly lose track of whether you are staying within your limits. You may think that shooting on video allows you to have an infinite ratio, but with video it's equally important to keep your shooting ratio down. Handing 30 hours of tapes to your editor for a 10-minute short isn't feasible. Neither is taking two days to get the one perfect take. Part of your role as director is to know when to call it a day, knowing that you may not have the perfect take, but you do have a usable one. Setting your ratio too low is also a problem. A 2:1 ratio due to lack of stock or time is not very realistic. It will severely limit the quality of your final film if you do not have enough coverage to work with when you come to edit. (See Rodriguez technique for how to shoot a 1:1 ratio.)

COVERAGE

How you cover a scene refers to the amount of takes and variety of shots you shoot for a particular scene. Shooting a scene with only two takes from one angle, then finding that only one of those takes is usable, means you have no coverage. However, having the same scene shot from multiple angles, including close ups and wide shots, means you have plenty of coverage.

Coverage is essential when it comes to editing a film; having enough takes and shots will give you multiple ways in which you can cut a scene together. Once you have shot a master scene or comprehensive take, you should try and cover the action from different angles, using as many different types or combinations of shot as you think it warrants. A film made with no coverage can appear visually stilted. To create a dynamic multi-dimensional edit, you need to shoot as much coverage as you can.

Master scene

Master scene is a technique that is common practice in filmmaking. It simply involves finding an angle from which you can cover the entire action of a scene, or as much as possible. Generally a wide shot, you film one or several takes of the entire scene. This then acts as a security, and you can shoot as much coverage as you like, knowing that you have already captured the entire scene and will be able to cut it in with the other shots and angles. Gaps are often not apparent until you reach the editing suite, and by then it's too late so shooting a master scene whenever possible is a wise precaution.

Overlap

When shooting multiple angles for a scene, it is vital that you overlap the action. Rather than shooting to the end of a line of dialogue and then starting another shot with the next line, you should always have at least a sentence or piece of movement from the tail end of the last shot. This gives you security and provides you with more leeway in the edit, as well as allowing the actors to develop the pace and rhythm of dialogue. Matching dialogue and movement between shots is vital for editing. A shot that has no common match point with a master scene or other coverage is generally unusable when it comes to editing.

Lines of direction

The line, crossing the line, or the 180-degree rule, is a technical consideration when it comes to the angles from which you choose to shoot a scene. If you have two actors, for instance, talking to each other in profile, then you imagine a straight line on which they are standing. The side of that line that you start filming from has to be the side you stay on to shoot any coverage. If you cross the line, when you cut the footage together, you would give the impression that the two actors had swapped positions. This is a rule that is often broken, and there is no reason why you shouldn't, if you think that a shot might work better by crossing the line.

The line is also the same principle that governs direction of movement. If you imagine that you were shooting an actor running down a street from one side of the road and then swapped to the other side of the road to get another shot, when you cut the shots together the actor would appear as if he was running back in the other direction.

CONTINUITY

Although many productions have a continuity supervisor, whose sole concern is to monitor continuity on set, it also pays for the director to be aware of continuity. Nearly all films are shot out of sequence using various shots to build up scenes, so maintaining continuity is vital to ensure they are usable. Actors' clothes and the position of props are obvious examples of things that need to be monitored. Shot lists can often require the same piece of action to be filmed again, much later in the day from a different angle, and although the order and placement of things might seem unforgettable immediately after a shot, recreating it hours later can be very taxing. Using digital stills cameras to monitor each shot as well as making notes or placing marks can all help avoid any continuity problems.

PROBLEM SOLVING

Translating an idea that you have in your head onto the screen is not always a straightforward process. Directing a film will always provide situations that you had not envisioned, whether this is literally a shot that can't be achieved in the way you had imagined it, or running out of time on a day's shoot. It is the director's job to find ways around these problems and spot them before they occur. Just as it takes imagination to think up the ideas in the first place, that imagination is also essential for finding creative ways to solve the problems in situ.

21. CREW

Organising the crew for your film requires you to understand not only the needs of your film, but also the demands of each role. Each member of the crew, in turn, must understand the roles of everybody else involved.

Ensuring that each head communicates with one another is crucial to an efficient team. For this complex group of people to function as a single unit, you need to impose a system and hierarchy. Even if everybody does a bit of everything on set, as is often the case on shorts, different areas of the production still need to be broken down into their separate departments. You will then need to designate specific roles to individuals; and if there is more than one person in a department then one should be head of that department (HOD).

This might seem like overkill on a small-scale production, but it really does make things faster and more efficient, as well as safer. A hierarchy will save everyone time and effort, and give people a specific purpose.

PRODUCTION MANAGER

The production manager is in charge of all the departments on the shoot. On shorts the producer often assumes this role. Having someone to coordinate all the practical elements on set is a necessity. If you don't have a producer on your film, then it is worth designating someone as production manager.

ASSISTANT DIRECTOR (AD)

The assistant director, or AD, is there to help the director get the job done, whether this is yelling commands such as 'action' and 'cut', ensuring the cast is ready for the next take, or keeping the crew up to date on what will be required for the next scene. Ultimately the AD should be able to have slightly more perspective on what is going on, both on and off the set, than the director, who will be concentrating on the actors and the DP. The AD uses this perspective to keep the shoot moving and should always be looking as far ahead as possible, allowing the director to focus on the job in hand.

CAMERA CREW

The DP is head of the camera crew and will also be in charge of the lighting and grip. Camera crews will normally consist of several assistants, and when shooting on film a focus puller and clapper loader. Gaffers and sparks will also look to the DP to give them instructions on where and how to place which lights. Grips will also take their instructions from the DP.

SOUND CREW

The sound department will usually consist of at least two people, the sound recordist or mixer (who is the HOD), and a boom pole operator. Although they are as vital as the camera crew, they often work around them rather than dictate their requirements.

GAFFERS/SPARKS

The amount of gaffers or sparks you have will depend on how much lighting you are using. The gaffer is normally the head of a team of sparks, who will deal with all the technical lighting needs of the shoot. Professional gaffers are trained electricians and their role and experience is crucial as far as lighting your set goes. They need to transfer the requests of the DP into feasible lighting set ups, involving power supplies, cabling, positioning and controlling of the lights. They work closely with the DP to achieve creative solutions for any shot or scene.

RIGGERS

Anything that involves building support structures, such as scaffolding towers, lighting rigs etc will be performed by trained riggers.

ART DEPARTMENT

The art department can range from one person to a massive team of set builders. Run by the art director or production designer, the role of the department is to assemble or dress the set as is required for a scene. On shorts the art department is often in charge of props as well. The art director will refer to the director, DP and continuity supervisor for instructions.

CONTINUITY SUPERVISOR

Continuity in a film is never a straightforward affair. The non-linear manner in which a shot list is assembled can make it very difficult to keep track of what should be where, or what should be on who. Simple errors with continuity can render entire portions of footage unusable. To avoid this, the continuity supervisor keeps careful notes on the script and storyboard, also noting what has been shot already, ensuring that the wardrobe and art departments maintain continuity.

COSTUME

A costume designer will often be in charge of sourcing outfits or making them. These outfits are then organised and maintained by the wardrobe department for the shoot. They ensure that the costumes are ready for particular scenes, and help the actors change into them. They'll also keep an eye on them while the shoot is in progress.

HAIR AND MAKE UP

The hair and make up departments will refer to the director and occasionally the DP. Make up and hairstyles should have been decided in pre-production, and performed at a reasonable interval before the actor is needed for a scene. Both need to be maintained while the shoot is in progress, so there are often two people in a department, one preparing and one on set, who is in charge of touch ups.

FINDING A CREW

How many people you need in your film crew really depends on the nature of your film. Using film crew databases and asking other filmmakers or producers for recommendations is the most straightforward approach to take. When hiring crew, whether they are offering their services free of charge or for a fee, it is important to find out what previous experience they have. CVs and showreels will indicate levels of expertise.

Figure 41. Shooting People website. www.shootingpeople.org

22. DIRECTOR OF PHOTOGRAPHY (DOP/DP)

The director of photography is also known as the DOP or just DP. More than just a camera operator, he or she controls the lighting, framing, composition and mood of your shots. The DP is in charge of trying to realise, as closely as possible, the shots that you want for your film, through the appropriate use of lenses, camera angles, lights and filters.

Deciding on who you want to shoot your film can be difficult. There is, of course, the option of shooting it yourself, and if you are planning on using a digital format such as DV or HDV then the technology is often straightforward enough for you to operate the camera with a minimum of experience. This way you retain complete control over what you are shooting. This may seem like a feasible solution in the planning stages, but there are several factors that you should bear in mind.

Although there are a lot of 'point and shoot' cameras on the market, these are intended for amateur and domestic use, and will inevitably produce much lower-quality images than professional equipment. This may well be an aesthetic you are after, and there is often a vibrancy to this kind of footage that simply can't be imitated on more professional cameras, but in general filmmakers tend to strive towards the highest possible quality image. If you are going to shoot on film or a high-quality video format, then you are really going to need someone who is more than just proficient with the technology, in order to maximise its potential.

On any film involving actors, as a director your time will mostly be spent blocking out the action and communicating what you want with them. On set or location, this will be your priority, and time will always be short. If you also need to make sure the camera is functioning properly and the lighting positioned effectively, then either the performance or the image may suffer. The more talent and experience a DP has, the better your film is going to look, which is why their role is such an important one. Whether you are shooting on DV or 35mm, you will be relying heavily on their skill to bring your ideas to life and this will give you the freedom to concentrate on directing.

To become a competent DP normally takes years of training, especially if they shoot on film. There are a lot more variables when shooting on S16 and 35mm than there are with digital formats. Professional DPs have usually worked their way through the camera assistant roles of clapper loader and focus puller, and once they have gained enough technical experience they concentrate on lighting before becoming a fully-fledged DP. Shooting on a digital format is often less labour-intensive and less technical than shooting on film, but, either way, your DP should be highly proficient at what you are asking them to do. Whatever format you are shooting on, you want to achieve the appropriate look without losing valuable time, or, potentially, losing shots.

It is imperative that as a director you are able to convey to the DP what type of visual style or look you are after. Otherwise you will both think you understand each other but actually have completely different ideas in mind. At this stage then you really need to have done your research. Try to gather together as much visual source material as you can. Whether a scene from a film, an advert, or a magazine photo, it will all be very useful when it comes to conveying your thoughts to a DP.

FINDING A DP

There are a number of ways to find a DP to shoot your short film. There's not much point in trying to persuade a highly-established DP to shoot a low-budget short film, because there's simply not a lot in it for them, so instead try and find someone who is both prepared and enthusiastic. The key to getting a good crew for your film is to find people that have as much to gain from it as you do.

The best places to start are film schools that run courses specifically for directors of photography. Film schools produce a lot of up and coming DPs every year, who will generally be keen to get involved in short film projects to gain more practical experience and put their training into practice. They are looking to showcase their talent and advance their skill and expertise. Try and find out when the end of year student screenings take place and go along to have a look at their work. Most colleges should be able to put you in touch with current or previous students and you can always put an ad up on the notice board.

Film industry databases on the Internet are also a good place to look, and will often have contact information. A lot of DPs will have their own websites with a list of credits and a downloadable showreel of their work. Budding DPs often work professionally as camera assistants on feature films and commercials, but relish short films as a chance to display their flair behind the camera.

Short film festivals are also a great place to find DPs. If you like the visual style of a film, there will usually be someone from the production there, who can put you in touch with the DP.

STYLE

Whoever you get to shoot your film, whether a professional or novice, always remember that the visual style of your film is one of the main areas in which it's possible to innovate and produce something highly original. Always check a potential DP's showreel and try and choose someone that shoots in a style you think will work for your film. Pay particular attention to their lighting and framing to see if this is compatible with the look that you want to achieve. Just as with any other role in filmmaking, a DP is constantly learning and no two shoots are ever the same. It's not always possible to recreate exactly what you want visually even at the best of times so be prepared to compromise and listen to your DP's advice along the way. On short films they will often be among the most experienced members of the crew.

INTERVIEW WITH SIMON MINETT (DP)

Simon Minett is an accomplished director of photography with over 15 years of experience in the film and television industries. Although he generally shoots commercials, music promos and corporates, he is also regularly involved in shooting short films. For further information about Simon Minett visit www.filmspace.net.

What are you in charge of in your capacity as a DP?

As DP, you direct photography. By interpreting the script and the director's ideas regarding the script into images, you make ideas that exist in the director's head into photographic reality.

At what stage of the pre-production do directors normally contact you? Is there an ideal time?

The ideal time is as much time as possible. The more time you can put into pre-production, the better the shoot is going to be. Unfortunately, there's often very little pre-production time with short films. Short films tend to be low-budget, but if people are working for nothing or for very little money, then at least pre-production is one element that's not going to cost very much!

Are you often involved in the decision process over which format to shoot on?

I'd expect to have some influence, but very often format is dictated by budget. If I feel strongly that a format is wrong for a job, then I think it's my job to say so, and I would hope that producers and directors would expect that from me.

What sort of preparation do you normally have to go through before shooting a short?

Discussions over format and meetings about storyboards. If it's a location shoot, then recces of locations and looking at photographs of locations. If it's a studio shoot, then having a look at the studio. I'd expect to have some involvement in procuring camera and lighting crew.

Whose job is it to put together camera, lighting and grip gear lists?

Working out what kind of camera, lighting and grip gear are going to be required

Figure 42. Simon Minett in action.

is very much the DP's role. If I'm working with people I trust, I'll often leave some of the minutiae of the lighting list to my lighting gaffer. We'll meet to discuss the main lighting requirements, and I'll let the gaffer fill in the blanks as regards all the lighting grip gear and stands etc. Again, with camera grip gear, I might just specify dolly and track, and let the grip work out all the accessories. Very rarely, I might get a camera assistant to expand a basic camera list, but only if I'm really up against it in terms of time.

If you're going to need camera assistants, is it up to the producer/director to find them for you or do you bring your own?

I would certainly attempt to find camera crew that I knew and trusted if possible. If I feel that the script is good enough to be worth putting some effort into, I will attempt to procure some or all of the camera crew and lighting crew, but I also have to bear in mind that pulling favours for people can't be done lightly because you're talking about people's time. If, as a DP, you do end up working with unknown crew the producer/director has found for you, it's worthwhile vetting them quite carefully, making sure that people can actually do what they say they can do. After all, it's a dangerous business, and some of the gear is worth a lot of money!

What format do you think is most viable for short filmmaking, with regards to achieving a high-quality cinematic image?

That's a Pandora's box of a question. There's no one answer. It depends on the nature of the project. The digital revolution is well underway and there are a variety of formats to choose from, but making that choice is very difficult, and it isn't only about money. A lot of people shoot short films on DV, but if a film is intended for festivals, and/or cinematic projection, then I think DV, or even HDV, is not the format. HDcam is a good format, but it's worth remembering it's only half the resolution of 16mm, and a quarter of the resolution of 35mm. Projected onto a cinema screen, the amount of image degradation at such low resolution is very apparent.

What format offers the most value for money?

I refer you to my last answer. On paper, shooting on film is a great deal more expensive than shooting digitally, but it's not just down to crunching the numbers. Film does still have a very particular aesthetic, which is currently to my mind still out-performing most digital technologies, apart from perhaps at the very high end, which is out of reach for most short filmmakers.

If you shoot on film, does that mean it will automatically look like films at the movies?

Not at all; that's entirely dependent upon the skills of the people making the film. A good crew can make a great film on a cheap camera; a poor crew can use very expensive equipment and end up with something absolutely dreadful.

What do you think is the most important aspect of being a good DP?

To be a communicator. To listen. To never forget that you're a facilitator; you're an artisan, not an artist, you're there to interpret other people's ideas, and make them reality.

Do all DPs have an individual style, or do you adjust to what the director wants?

Difficult question. Obviously DPs do develop styles, and do have quirks and tricks that they end up using, but I think that as a DP one should aim to be a chameleon, to replicate any look, or to interpret ideas in any way that the director wants to interpret them. I would always shy away from being pigeon-holed as having a particular look.

What kinds of thing can go wrong, camera-wise, on a short film shoot?

Short films, as we said before, tend on the whole to be low-budget, and as a result there is financial pressure on all the departments. It's very common to have inexperienced crew on short films, and so mistakes get made. This is particularly acute in relation to camera crew, as any mistakes can be absolutely catastrophic. If an art director or a wardrobe or make up person makes a mistake it can usually be dealt with somehow in post-production, perhaps by re-editing in some way, but if, for example, the focus puller makes a mistake, that's that, you've got to re-shoot; all the material is simply unusable. This is especially true when shooting on 35mm, when focus pulling becomes absolutely crucial because of the shallow depth of field.

How can the producer/director make your life easier as a DP?

Allow enough time in pre-production. All the pieces need to be in place before you start shooting; that includes post-production. It's very important for your producer/director to have their post-production workflow worked out before turn over, because that can affect how you shoot. It's crucial. Is the job going to go for projection? Is it just for TV? Is a telecine necessary or will it be traditional film grading? Etc, etc.

What are the commonest misconceptions you encounter working with a director?

Directors come in all shapes and sizes; some are more experienced, some are less. The one crucial skill that a director must have is the skill to communicate, to translate their ideas into a language the film crew can understand. I don't expect a director to necessarily be conversant with cinematographic language; I don't mind if the director can't say 'we need to track left, pan right, crane down', but they have to be able to tell me how they want it to look in some way I can interpret. If the director is less experienced, the role of the DP is to fill the gaps with regards to how the film gets shot; but you've also got to know when to step back.

Once the shoot is over, are you also involved in the post-production processes such as grading etc?

Especially with digital technology being more and more prevalent, I increasingly think that shooting a film is only half of the issue photographically. In a way, grading is an extension of what the DP does. Although it's very often impossible, due to money and time restrictions, a DP's input into post-production can be very useful, and it shouldn't be assumed that the end of the shoot is the end of the DP's role. At worst, a DP may have shot in a particular way for a particular look, and if nobody has communicated this to the grader then they may go against it in grading and end up in trouble.

What about using short ends and re-cans? Can you shoot a film on them?

It is possible to shoot a film on film extremely cheaply on short ends and re-cans. The most important thing is to get them clip tested by the laboratory to make sure that they haven't broken down so that the colour balance has shifted. Same with tape stock. No reason why you can't re-use tape stock, but it's well worth re-blacking all the tapes, to make sure there's no drop-out on them. Ideally, if you've got the money, you don't do that, but often people need to save money.

What kind of lights should you use? Do you use different lights for shooting on film and video?

I don't see a distinction between lighting for film and lighting for digital; it's all lighting and it depends on the project. The point is to plan what you'll need for a particular scene and why you need it, working within budget. If you can't afford your first choice, then how can you get around that? Always find an imaginative way to use whatever money's available. If you've got a big wide shot at night you may need a lot of lighting equipment. If it's daylight exterior, you may need very little indeed. People will often use smaller lighting kits for digital format, but it's not the case that digital formats automatically need less lighting. In fact, to my mind, they need more, because they're less light-sensitive.

What are key light, backlight, and fill used for? Do you only need three lights?

Three-point lighting is taught as the classic way to light a three-dimensional object. Key light, we speak of as the motivating light source. Fill light controls the contrast ratio. Mood is established by fill. Backlight, or rim light, makes objects stand out from the background and appear more three-dimensional.

Can you use old film cameras, because they're cheaper, or do you have to shoot on brand new ones?

One of the most wonderful aspects of shooting on film is that the technology is in the film stock. Film images essentially come down to the lens in front of the film and the film stock, and film stock has improved massively, far outstripping any of the digital technologies. There's no reason at all why you can't shoot on an old camera and, providing the camera's in good condition, get a good result.

Can you shoot a whole film on a zoom lens?

Absolutely. Classic case in point is a BAFTA award-winning short called *About a Girl* shot by Jeff Boyle. Prime lenses are better; they are slightly higher resolution, there's less glass. But if you're working on higher-resolution format, there's no reason why you can't work with a zoom at all.

What advice do you have for new short film directors?

Make sure you know what you want to do with your film before you shoot it. Get a crew around you who you know can do the job. Don't try and do what can't be achieved within the budget; keep it simple.

How long do you think it will be before people stop shooting on film?

I don't think film will disappear overnight. Film is expensive and digital technologies will become more prevalent, but film will remain for a long, long time to come.

Why might you need to use different stocks? Can you use daylight stock indoors, and vice versa?

As a DP, different film stocks are like different paints for an artist. Stocks can be used in an unusual way to get a particular effect. Using high ASA stocks to get a grainy effect, using low-ASA stocks to get a grain-free effect; using stocks of a particular colour temperature in a deliberately different environment in order to get a particular colour bias. Manipulation of stock is a very important and useful part of the DP's armoury.

Can most problems be fixed in post-production? Which can't be?

The things you can't fix in post are the in-camera elements of shooting. Has the film been loaded correctly? Is it in focus? Has it been exposed correctly? If there's a rip perf (perforation) on a piece of film that goes into the lab, the whole bath can be ruined. All the rushes will simply be destroyed. Focus has to be there or you're never going to get it back. Very often, inexperienced DPs get the exposure wrong. If you're on film or high-resolution format that can be fixed in post, but it depends on what post-production you have, what resolution you have in post-production.

Is it possible to shoot and direct at the same time?

Yes, depending on genre. With dramatic cinematography it's unlikely, because there's too much to do. That's not to say people don't do it, but it's not really viable to be able to deal with actors and deal with cinematography at the same time.

Why do you need camera assistants?

If they know what they're doing, a camera assistant is a really useful resource. The more time the DP has to spend dealing with logistics, the less time they're going to have to devote to the interpretation of ideas. Regular camera assistants make the shoot go quicker, and give the DP more freedom to create an aesthetic.

What do you enjoy most about working on short films?

Short films can be extremely creative. There's a certain freedom, they're good for the soul.

23. LOCATION SOUND

The importance of recording high-quality location sound cannot be stressed enough. Although digital sound engineering now offers filmmakers more precise control and opportunity for manipulation and processing, to make use of this potential an initially clean and consistent recording is required.

Location or production sound is the process of recording the dialogue of the actors as well as sound effects and atmosphere. This crucial role is performed by the sound department, which usually consists of a sound mixer and boom operator.

SOUND MIXER

The sound mixer is responsible for monitoring and mixing the levels of various sources of audio and also deciding how those sources should be recorded, which type of microphone should be used and how they should be placed. The sound mixer also coordinates the rest of the sound team.

BOOM OPERATOR

The boom operator is the sound mixer's assistant, responsible for placing the microphones on the actors or set, as well as directly controlling a microphone attached to the end of a boom pole.

TECHNIQUE

How a scene can be optimally recorded depends on the nature of the set or location and the demands of the shot. There is no single method of recording that will cover all eventualities, so a combination of techniques is often used.

Boom

Using a boom generally allows for a greater amount of control when recording dialogue. The basic principle is that a directional microphone is attached to an extendable pole, often a professional fisher pole that allows the pole to be extended or contracted, or a fixed-length fish pole. The boom operator is then able to follow the movements of the actors, while keeping the microphone out of the shot. Directional microphones are generally used for this purpose, as they can be aimed at the actors, focusing on picking up the dialogue rather than the extraneous sounds.

Planted

When a specific shot does not allow for a boom operator to follow the action, or the actors remain static, a planted microphone can be used, often hidden behind a prop or piece of scenery.

On body

Small microphones known as clip-on or lavalier microphones can be attached to the clothing of the individual actors and then either attached to the mixer via cables, or a radio microphone can be used. Lavalier microphones have the advantage of being small and concealable, but the disadvantage of picking up additional sounds, such as the rustle of an actor's costume or gestures.

Room tone/atmos

Although the focus of the sound crew is generally the dialogue, it's also standard to record just the sound or atmosphere of a particular location or set. This helps to fill any gaps that can occur editing.

EQUIPMENT

Just like film camera and lighting equipment, professional sound equipment is complex to set up and operate, relying on both technical know-how and experience as to which methods and approaches are best for various situations.

Choices over types of microphone, mixer and whether to record straight to the audio channels of the video camera or on a separate format such as DAT all need to be weighed up by the sound recordist based on the demands of your film. If you want to get dialogue of professional quality for your film then ideally you should try and find an experienced sound recordist, or at least someone with knowledge of sound recording. Both should be able to choose the right combination of microphones and mixer for the situation.

INTERVIEW WITH OLI COHEN (SOUND RECORDIST)

Oli Cohen is a sound recordist who recorded his first short film over ten years ago. He is based in London but has worked and travelled all over the UK and around the world. Having an understanding and experience of both location and post-production sound, as well as a love for filmmaking, Oli has worked on numerous features, documentaries, commercials, corporates, webcasts, EPKs, art projects and award-winning short films. For further information about Oli Cohen visit www. olicohen.com.

How did you become a sound recordist?

Coming from a background in classical music, I was trained from a young age to listen in a very focused way. As a teenager in the late 80s and 90s, I was very much into Hi-Fi, like many people. I also played in numerous guitar bands, but the breakthrough really came when I bought my first sampler. I became enchanted by the ability to record and manipulate any sound and it was this, along

Figure 43. Oli Cohen in action.

with a love for films and documentaries, which led me to working with sound professionally. The first thing I ever did was volunteer as a sound assistant on a student short film at the Northern Film School up in Leeds. Within a short space of time I was sound recording on shorts but I didn't really know what I was doing so I decided to apply to the National Film and Television School (NFTS), where I ended up studying screen sound, both location and post, for three years.

What essentially are you in charge of when working on a film?

As a sound recordist it is your responsibility to get the best possible, usable, appropriate sound for each shot and scene. Ultimately, this means capturing the dialogue as cleanly as possible.

At what stage of a production do you normally get involved? Is there an ideal time?

Ideally you get involved early so that you can go on recces, meet other heads of department, find a boom operator who's available and plan your life a bit. In reality, however, with short films I normally get a call a couple of days before shooting starts.

Do you get consulted about potential locations?

Very rarely. Often with shorts there's so much begging and scraping going on that people can't afford to be that choosy. This of course can result in some dodgy sound locations, like recording right under the flight pass near Heathrow!

It has been said that location sound is always a compromise. Well, it certainly was on that film.

Do you get to pick what equipment you want to use for a film?

I always use my own kit on short films. This saves a lot of hassle for everyone, especially me.

How do you get an idea of what equipment might be needed?

I have a standard kit that I always bring along. On drama it makes sense to record the sound separately, onto either DAT or Hard Disc, and you have to do this if they're shooting on film. On commercials shot on HD, or with documentaries, I usually record straight to camera, which can make life easier in post, so a decision has to be made about what you're recording on. The other main consideration is how many characters are talking and how many personal mics you're going to need; so you need to read the script. If there are loads of characters, which is rarely the case on shorts, then you might also need a larger mixer.

Are you responsible for picking and prepping the gear for a shoot?

Before I bought my own equipment I would always pick up and prep the sound equipment. The way I see it, it's part of the job as a head of the sound department to make sure that all the kit is working. I would never want to turn up on a job without having gone through the kit only to realise that something essential, like a cable, was missing. It's too stressful and you could lose half a day's shooting.

Can you record all the sound on your own or do you need assistants?

Depending on the shoot, it is possible to record the sound on your own but essentially you would be doing the work of two people so it's not to be advised. The sound would also be compromised, as there's only so much balancing you can do when you're boom operating at the same time and only so much you can carry! Without a boom operator it's tempting to rely more on radio mics but they quite simply don't sound as good and they come with all kinds of problems.

How many people are normally in the sound recording crew and who's in charge?

The sound crew normally consists of two people, the sound recordist or mixer, and a boom operator. On larger productions there's normally a third man. The sound recordist is head of the department but the work should be more of a collaboration in my opinion, as opposed to the sound recordist telling the boom op what to do. As a sound recordist you want to listen, mix and record, as well as making notes, rather than checking up on your boom op. Decent boom operators know what to do anyway. They know where to place the boom mic, they are ahead in finding out what's going on, they understand the importance of pulling the mic back if one of the characters starts shouting and they help pack up when moving location etc. The problem is, you rarely get experienced boom operators working on short films.

What kind of skills do you need to be a good sound recordist?

Being able to listen critically, and to be able to hear and understand the difference between a decent recording and a not so good one helps. Obviously you need to know how to use the equipment. It's certainly useful if you like gadgets. An overall knowledge of filmmaking is of course important and it also helps if you understand the post-production process and can think in terms of editing a scene together. As with any job on set it's important to have decent people skills and not to get too precious about what you're doing, but rather to remember that ultimately you're there to help the director achieve what he or she wants.

What kind of kit would you normally take on a small budget short film?

On a small budget short film the kit I normally use consists of the following:

Sennheiser HD 25 Headphones
SQN-4S MK IVe mixer
Tascam DAP1 Dat Machine
Sennheiser 416 shotgun microphone with full Rycote Kit
Neuman TLM 103 microphone (used for voiceovers)
Mini Panamic Boom Pole
Maxi Panamic Boom Pole
2 x 2020 Audio Ltd Radio Kits with Sanken Cos 11s
An excessive supply of 9 volt batteries
48v Phantom Power Cable for the TX2020
2 x U 100 Audio Technica Radio Kits with MT830Rs + AT899s
(these are also sometimes used as directors' comms)

Hawkwoods APR1 adaptor, which is used to power everything

2 x Hawkwoods NP65 Li-Ion batteries

1 Hawkwoods NP-29 Ni-Cad battery

1 Hawkwoods MR4 Multi-Chemistry Battery Charger

KT Systems bag + harness

3 x Microphone Stands

Magic Arm + Stand

Peli Cases

2 stools

2 x 10 metre and 2 x 5 metre XLR cable

All kinds of connectors

Carpet (to quieten footsteps that are out of shot)

Toupee tape, plaster tape and other accessories for attaching radio mics

Radio mic pouches and belts

All kinds of other accessories such as wasp spray, head torch, tessa tape to quieten shoes, warm clothes and waterproofs, sound report sheets, envelopes and multiple pens, cable ties and leatherman.

Why are there different types of microphone?

Different types of microphone have different applications. In a music studio scenario you wouldn't want to use the same type of microphone to mic up a punchy loud sound, like a kick drum, as a quiet delicate one, like a breathy vocal. Different types of microphone also have different pick up patterns. On film sets the most common types of microphone used, attached to the end of boom poles, are directional shotgun microphones, though supercardioid non-shotgun mics, which are also strongly directional, can also be used. Directional microphones allow the capsule to be somewhat further away but they do need to be pointing at the sound source. Personal mics, which tend to be omni directional, are also very frequently used on drama. These are hidden on the actors and connected to some sort of radio link. They're particularly useful for wide shots and other times when you can't get the boom in.

Are there any that you can use in all circumstances?

Not really. The most important mic to have though is a shotgun mic. They're reliable and can be used in most circumstances.

What are the basic techniques you might use to record a scene?

With short films there seems to be no standard way of shooting a scene as often filmmakers want to experiment but I do have a basic approach to sound recording that seems to work quite well which is, if it moves record it. Exceptions to this are when the camera is recording slow motion at a higher frame rate and it's making too much noise or when the director has specifically insisted that it's a mute shot.

When a situation isn't immediately obvious, it's sometimes worth stopping a moment and just thinking what is really important to hear for this particular shot and how should it sound and then go from there. On a single close up shot it's obvious to focus on the person in frame talking and the boom mic should be on that character but, if it's not too much hassle, it might also be worth getting the off-screen dialogue of the person they're talking to, perhaps with the radio mic that's already on them, as an additional editing option, even though you know that they're going to come round and shoot the reverse. What's really important is that the boom mic and the radio mics should not be mixed together but should rather be split onto different tracks. If this isn't done, a perfectly acceptable boom track might be spoilt by something like an actor knocking his personal microphone or some strange off-screen breathing.

What's the most common way of recording a scene?

It all depends on how it's being shot and what's happening in that scene. If the scene's being shot handheld or on steadicam and we're outside and there's lots of movement, I'd be inclined to mic up the talking characters. In more standard interior scenes you can often get everything on the boom. A classic way of shooting is to start with the master wide and then to go in for two shots and close ups. On the master wide you could just get a general recording with perspective, knowing that you can get the more intimate close recordings when the camera goes in. It's useful here to think about the wide recording and the closer recordings editing together. Some would say it's best not to get too close and keep some kind of perspective but others argue that the dialogue should be recorded as clean and close as possible – after all you can always make it sound further away in post. I think there are too many variables to make any hard and fast rules here, like the size of the room, the microphone you're using, how good a radio mic is sounding or how loud the actor is talking. But if in doubt, get closer with the mic and listen carefully.

Why do you use a boom pole?

Using a microphone on the end of a boom pole is the best way to get decent audio on a film set. The pole enables the operator to get the microphone in an appropriately close position to the actor. Normal practice is to have the pole in front of and above the actor's head pointing down as that's where the top of the frame is and it's out of the way. Sometimes it's necessary to go from underneath, which is fine.

How long does it take to get set up to record a scene?

That depends on the particular sound team. From opening my case I can be set up to record in seconds. Everything is always connected. But putting personal mics on can be a little time consuming and fiddly and finding the right moment can also prove difficult. Ideally the sound department should never keep on set waiting so it's best to be ahead of the game and to be efficient and organised, knowing where everything is. It's important to keep your best cards for when you really need them and not to hold people up unnecessarily.

If you are recording dialogue, do you have to know the script?

Knowing the script helps, especially as regards balancing multiple radio mics, but it's particularly important for the boom operator to know the script. As a boom operator I used to remember the last word a character would say before moving the mic towards the next person.

Do you have to log all the different takes that you record?

Yes, you do. Comments like 'end board' make life a lot easier in post as well. Having worked as a sound editor, I also know it's useful to have a little description of the shot and scene when looking for words from alternative takes.

Why do you have to record a take of just ambience (presence) as well as the dialogue?

Having an atmos track where there is no movement at all is a very useful thing from a sound editing point of view. In an intimate dialogue scene, for example, to make the dialogue work smoothly a sound editor might want to get rid of a distracting breath or a clothing move in between the dialogue. Chopping it out is the easy bit but it has to be filled and finding a matching bit of sound from somewhere else can prove difficult. That's why room tones and the like are recorded. But it's difficult to get a whole crew to be silent so I tend to do atmos tracks only when I feel they're really necessary or when there's no or little crew around. For these types of recordings, the microphone should be in a similar position to where it was during the actual shooting of the scene and all the same lights should be on.

Do you record sound effects too?

Yes, I record sound effects as well, but would never want to do it at the expense of holding the whole production up unless it was absolutely necessary. In a restaurant scene, for example, I would want all the background characters not to be making any noise during the shooting of the dialogue and then afterwards I'd record the sound of background chat. What I wouldn't do is record all the other sounds you might hear in a restaurant as these can easily be sourced from a library, or created in a foley session, and I wouldn't want to use up valuable production time. Other sounds, whether they're general atmospheres or specific effects, I might go off and record away from the rest of the shoot.

If you think that you didn't get a clean recording for a take, what do you do?

If it's an appalling take from both a performance and camera point of view, and the sound was also spoilt by a plane, for example, I won't bother saying anything, as there's no point. Most of the time, though, everyone can hear the plane or the siren that's gone off in the middle of the shot so they look at me and see me shaking my head and the director will yell cut. If that doesn't happen and I'm the only one who knows it wasn't a decent enough recording then I would say straight away.

Do you ever add effects like reverb in the mix while you are recording?

No. Adding effects, like reverb, is something you would not want to do. It's best to record in a way that will allow more, rather than less, creative freedom in post-production. In an editing room, or a dubbing theatre, you're in a far better situation to decide how to treat a sound. The most I might do is add a bit of bass cut.

Do different post-production workflows require different techniques for the location sound recording?

Yes, they do. My recommendation is that if you want to do something a bit more complicated, like recording stereo sound in M+S, or recording on multiple tracks of audio, then it's worth having a chat with the picture and sound editors.

Some editors might only want a two-channel mix as they don't want the hassle of dealing with multiple tracks of separate audio.

Is it now possible to fix any location sound recording problems in post-production?

NO. It's definitely a mistake to go down the 'it can be fixed in post' route. In a similar way, when you take a photograph it's best to take a decent photograph to begin with, rather than thinking 'I'll tweak it in Photoshop later'. Yes, all kinds of things can be done to improve how something sounds and with effort it's sometimes possible to make a dodgy recording usable, but you can never turn it into a decent recording. Turning a decent recording into something more dirty, on the other hand, is quite easy. Similarly, you can make a close recording sound more distant but you certainly can't effectively make a distant recording sound close. When there's a serious problem with the location sound – for example, there might be a rain machine used on a certain scene – then you have little choice but to record everything again in an ADR session, using the location sound as a guide.

Are you involved in the post-production? Do you record ADR as well?

I've worked as a sound editor in post-production a fair amount and have attended a number of ADR sessions, sometimes as a recordist but usually as a dialogue editor. This is certainly not usual though.

What are the most common problems you encounter when trying to record a scene?

The most common problems include clothing rustle on personal mics, having a boom operator who doesn't know what they're doing, hearing sirens, planes or other loud vehicles, and recording in extreme weather conditions. Noisy generators and HMI lights are often problematic as well. Also, actors sometimes have a tendency to speak too quietly which can be a problem. Similarly, in nightclub scenes and other loud situations, it's hard for them to remember to raise their voices and express themselves as you might if it was actually loud.

What can the producer or director do to make your life easier on a film?

The director doesn't really need to do anything, I'm here to make his or her life easier, but it's always a good idea to wait just a bit longer before calling cut though. Those extra seconds can make a dialogue edit a lot smoother. But by far the most important thing that makes my life easier on set is to have a decent boom operator. Being sent the latest script with scene and page numbers also helps a lot, as well as unit lists and an easy to read call sheet that clearly says what time call time is and where it is. Quiet locations are great too.

How would you go about finding a sound recordist for a short film?

The best way is through recommendation, so ask around. Alternatively, there are all kinds of websites and resources on the Internet for short filmmakers. Or you could approach a film school.

What advice do you have for inexperienced people considering recording the sound for a short?

Get some experience as a boom operator or sound assistant first.

Only consider using professional equipment.

Don't rely on meters. You always have to listen.

Keep your best cards for when you really need them.

Remember you are there to help the director achieve their vision.

If it moves record it.

Make sure you get on with the first AD.

If you make a mistake admit it straightaway.

Don't turn up on set expecting the kit to work without having gone through it first.

Make sure you have a surplus amount of stock and batteries.

Think what the important sound is for each shot and how the scene will be cut together.

Watch, and listen to, lots of movies.

What do you enjoy most about working on short films?

There's nearly always a good atmosphere on set. People are doing if for the love of it or they're there to learn. There's little room for overly cynical or jaded people. Everyone tends to be coming from a positive place and are into doing something quite cool. It's great to be involved in actually making something, especially something that requires a great deal of collaboration. I also enjoy both the technical and creative side of filmmaking as well as its constant variety.

24. POST-PRODUCTION WORKFLOW

Workflow refers to the series of technical steps your film needs to go through in post-production for it to be completed. This includes everything that you have to do to turn your raw footage into a finished film on a screening format, so the processes and changes in format that are involved in moving the footage between these stages as well as the order you do them in.

Different productions will have different needs, for example a film shot on 16mm will require development and transfer, while a DV production won't, but might require complex computer effects etc.

So workflows differ greatly depending on the nature of the project and can be complicated or easy to plan depending on the specific needs of a film.

Because different formats have specific technical qualities, your workflow will, to a certain extent, be decided by which format you choose to shoot on, so it is something that should be planned during pre-production.

Even though your workflow will be governed by your format, due to the amount of variety available in the technical post-production of films there is still a huge choice in the systems and processes that workflows can consist of and often several different ways of getting from start to finish.

When choosing a workflow, it is important that you try and find one that is right for the needs of your film. Choosing the right workflow and sticking to it will enable you to complete your film smoothly and efficiently.

Potential workflows for your film will generally be governed by two factors, budget and quality.

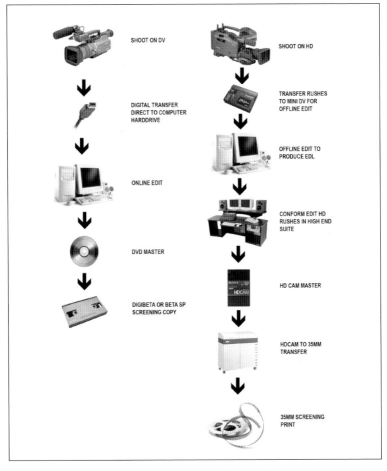

Figure 44. Diagram of common digital workflows.

QUALITY PRESERVATION

The golden rule of following a workflow process is quality preservation. Within reason you should never lose anything other than a reasonable margin of quality through your workflow, unless it is absolutely unavoidable.

Most workflows result in several transfers taking place and this is where a potential for quality loss occurs along the way. Whether you need to transfer DV footage from a camera to a computer for editing, or footage on a hard drive between computers, you need to make sure that the transfer itself and the systems you are transferring to will maintain the resolution of your initial footage.

Workflows are only as strong as their weakest link. Quality lost at any stage will be passed along and affect the final quality of your film. So you need to plan a workflow that will preserve the initial resolution that you started with.

BUDGET

It's vital that you treat the decisions over workflow realistically in terms of your budget. When initially choosing a format to shoot on, you need to not only evaluate the quality and cost of that format, but also the type of workflow it entails. This may seem straightforward enough, but the higher the quality of your post-production workflow the higher the expenses involved will generally be.

25. EDITING

In the process of shooting your script, you will have broken down scenes into individual shots and those shots into takes, resulting in footage that should cover all the material you needed, but probably not in an order resembling the script. The first step of editing is to reassemble your footage into the structure and sequence of the original story. This will provide you with a basis to begin giving your film pace and form. Editing can be an extremely creative process that gives you the chance to revise your initial story and how it's told, as well as create nuances and details that can define how the audience perceives what is occurring.

Whether you straightforwardly recreate the composition of your script, or drastically edit it into a different form, your options and decisions will be governed by the amount of coverage you shot. It's often said that you learn filmmaking in the edit, for no matter how well you have planned and choreographed your shoot, you will often find yourself wishing you had shot a bit more. Coverage really is the most vital contingent for editing; having close ups, wide shots and general coverage of action from different angles will multiply the possibilities that you have during editing and will allow you to create a finished version that is both visually dynamic and well-balanced.

Just like any other area of short filmmaking, there are no rules as to how you should edit a short; it's up to you to rely on instinct and creativity to resolve how the material is best portrayed.

NON-LINEAR (NLE)

Non-linear refers to the way in which most contemporary editing is performed.

It's a process that allows you to create an edit by accessing the source material at any given point and the possibility to start putting it together from any point. By giving you a virtual timeline, clips can be dragged and dropped onto it at any point and shifted around indefinitely. This means you don't need to build your edit by beginning at the start and working your way through to the end. Linear editing necessitates working through from the first shot to the last, but non-linear gives you the freedom to, for instance, start building your film from the middle outwards.

All contemporary editing systems are non-linear; they are digitally-based, allowing the footage to be stored on hard drives and retrieved quickly and efficiently. Based largely on the same principles of organisation and assembly as those developed by editors working directly with real film negatives, modern editing software allows you to work fluidly and precisely.

Time code

Non-linear editing was partially made possible by the invention of time code. Time code consists of data information that relates directly to the footage you are working with, consisting of hour, minute, second and frame references, allowing the footage to be identified and synchronised within an editing system or other post-production processes. It is often generated or added to the video footage during the actual recording and then provides a universal reference throughout the post-production of the film. There are many different forms of time code; the most common and widely used within filmmaking is SMPTE. This SMPTE time code can be read by the editing system and used as a reference for anyone from the editor to the soundtrack composer.

CHOOSING AN EDITING SYSTEM

There are several considerations when it comes to choosing a digital editing system.

If using editing software that can be used on a domestic computer, you need to ensure that the software can work with the footage at the desired resolution and that the computer can store and process that amount of digital information.

Both Final Cut Pro and Adobe Premiere are available in versions that can process both standard-definition and high-definition resolutions. This means that you can perform extremely high-quality editing with them, whether this is online or offline. Most high-end home computers will have enough processing power and external storage solutions to be able to work with lower-resolution compressed formats, allowing you to perform an online edit without any trouble, and this is by far the best solution for most lower-resolution projects.

To work with uncompressed high-definition footage, however, you will need an extremely powerful computer and serious storage capacity to perform online edits and this is where you will probably need to use a post-production facility for editing and conforming.

All the major digital software programmes work on the same concept. They allow you to capture and log your source footage, which can be broken down into clips and organised and stored in bins, from where they can be arranged into sequences on a virtual timeline. As long as the software can technically perform what you are asking of it, then the one you find most comfortable to work with is the best for you.

Editing is a time-consuming process, so hiring gear or time at post-production facilities becomes very expensive. The ideal is to find a system that gives you as much time to work with as possible and know well enough to work easily with.

One of the most important breakthroughs in filmmaking is workflows that are self-contained on one system. The process of making films used to require transfers, multiple processes, systems and locations to get the film to a completed stage. All of which was time-consuming, labour-intensive and expensive. This has all changed. With most digital formats it is now possible to use one or several programmes on a single computer that you can perform nearly your entire workflow on. Most NLE computer-editing packages will allow you to edit both image and sound, create titles and credits, add transition effects and perform colour correction, all within the one programme. If your project requires that elements be worked on in other programmes, such as soundtrack composition or visual effects, then the most important consideration is whether the programmes are compatible and the format of files you are working on can be shared between the programmes easily.

Figure 45.
Final Cut Pro editing program.

Intuitive editing

Software editing programmes are designed to be versatile; they have been developed for all kinds of projects and the demands that go with them. The result is programmes that let you work in a very simple fashion if the project requires it, or in a very complex technical way if that's what is required. Simple commands such as splicing a clip or creating a dissolve can be done in a variety of ways, so there is often no single way or right way to do most tasks.

Most programmes offer about six different ways to do everything, but you don't have to learn all of them, it's simply a case of finding which one is most straightforward and practical for you.

Methodical editing

The amount of footage that you shoot for any project, compared to how much actually makes it into the final edit can be vast. Depending on your shooting ratio, you will often be dealing with hours of rushes from which you will create a film that might only be a few minutes long. Dealing with this amount of material has the potential for chaos; spending hours trawling through your footage looking for a few seconds of material that you want to use is not uncommon. The key to avoiding this type of scenario really comes down to taking an organised and methodical approach when capturing, logging and naming your footage. Taking the time to break down your footage into individual takes, with names and numbers, often seems like a painstaking process when what you really want to do is get straight into editing it, but in the long term it allows you to work much faster and more efficiently.

Working with an editor

Editing used to be a process that was carried out in suites at post-production facilities. Individual editing systems required highly-skilled operators to use them. Traditionally, feature film directors hardly ever edit their films and often only work alongside professional editors. With the advent of increasingly powerful and sophisticated software systems that can be used on home computers, however, there is now a vast amount of amateur filmmakers who shoot and edit their own films. But, choosing to work with someone who is

Figure 46.
Selection of transition effects on *Adobe Premiere*.

either a professional or experienced amateur editor has several benefits. The first is that you can rely on their technical expertise to operate the software. The second and most important is that you benefit from their experience and talent. Even if you end up making the majority of the editorial choices, having another set of eyes, and someone skilled enough to present you with different possibilities, can only make your film better.

CUTS AND TRANSITIONS

The basic processes of editing are choosing the length of the individual clips and judging the precise moment at which one finishes and the next begins. This cutting point or junction between two clips can be handled in a variety of ways. Cuts between clips can be subtle, whereby the passage of time within a scene is maintained, and cuts or edit points become almost subliminal for the viewer. By maintaining the passage of time through a scene the filmmaker is often able to guide the viewer through a scene without them really being aware of the edit points. This is achieved not only by maintaining a natural timeline but also by choice of shots. Again, coverage is crucial for this style of editing, as its subtlety is often achieved by moving in and out of the scene incrementally. So for example, cutting from a wide to a medium shot and then to a close up will often be less of a noticeable edit than cutting straight from a wide shot to a close up, or vice versa; having a variety of angles and types of shot allows the editor more options in shifting the viewpoint in small unnoticeable steps rather than leaps. The other technique used to achieve seamless editing is cutting on the action. Using a movement within a scene as an edit point is ideal for convincing editing. Two different shots that contain the same action can be aligned on different video tracks and then a point within the action chosen to cut between them. An ubiquitous use of this technique within film is a character opening a door: a shot of a character from behind opening a door is cut with a reverse angle shot from the other side of the door where we see the character emerging. If you aligned these two shots and cut from the moment before the door was actually opened to the reverse angle with the door being opened, the result would be an edit that followed the series of events in real time, but may appear abrupt. However, if you chose a point at which the door was already partially open and then cut to the reverse at the moment the door was at the same angle, the momentum of the action would create a very subtle edit. This use of action and reaction is often the basis of smooth and dynamic editing. However, the timing and abruptness of a cut can also be used to great effect. A specific sequence or scene might benefit from this type of editing, to jolt the audience from one shot to another, such as a wide shot straight to an extreme close up. The passage of time can also be manipulated; cutting away the middle portion of a shot will create a jump cut, which can be used to emphasise the unreal quality of film time. Transitions such as dissolves and fades are also often employed to create the illusion of time passing and create a softer shift from scene to scene.

Rough cut

A rough cut is the first basic edit that you produce. This means that you will have captured all your footage and assembled it into the structure of the original script again. Working from your storyboard and script as reference you can begin to place your shots in sequence, choosing the best takes as you go and laying down a basic structure that will give you your first idea of how your film will actually look on the screen. This is generally the best time to test screen the film to other people; constructive feedback from people may well give you insight into which parts of the film are working or need to be worked on.

Offline

Offline editing is the editing of a copy of the master footage on another format (normally lower-resolution) and often on another editing system; it's a common step in many post-production workflows.

Offlines are copies of your film taken from the master format, whether digital or film. The quality of offlines is not generally as important as the master copy because they are designed for editing only to create the EDL information, so that either a conform edit of the final cut version or a neg cut can then take place. The actual offline material never gets screened and is a dead-end version.

Offline editing is used to both cut the costs of a production and make the editing process faster and easier. For instance, if you have shot your film on S16 or 35mm then you don't want to actually splice and assemble an edit with the actual negative; this would be painstaking, time-consuming and potentially damage the negative, so a telecined version on a DV format would be produced. This version can be edited on a computer-based editing system much more quickly and efficiently.

Even films that have been shot on a digital format, if they are very high-resolution, will often have lower-resolution offline versions made for editing; the processes and systems that can handle the high-resolution are often extremely expensive to use, and there is simply no need to complete the editing stage at the full resolution of the original version.

Online

Online editing is working with the film at its full resolution. Whether this is the original format or not, this online version is the one that will actually end up producing the screening copy. Online editing can be performed for an entire project; for example shooting a film on MiniDV, loading it on to a computer for editing and then exporting it back to MiniDV would be an entirely online edited version. Or an online edit can also take place after an offline, so for instance a film shot on HD might be edited offline on a domestic computer with a DV version of the footage to produce a rough cut, then the EDL could be used to recreate the edit in an HD editing suite to finetune the project and produce the final edit for exporting back out to an HD format. With projects that have been shot on a lower-resolution format like DV, there is often no need for an offline version, so the entire editing process is online.

CLIPS AND FILES

When working on a digital editing system, your footage will be stored digitally as files. Just like videotape formats there are a huge amount of digital file types, and just like digital tape formats they all involve encoding and compression (see video). These file systems act as containers for portions of encoded media, with many of them capable of containing both visual and audio information. These files use a variety of codecs to encode and store the data, often giving you the choice of what type of codec you want to use. The reason why there are so many different file types and codecs is because they are all designed for different purposes. Streaming a video over the net requires small files that have to be highly compressed for that amount of data to be transferred fast enough. Correcting a still image in Photoshop will require a large high-resolution file type so that there is the maximum amount of image information to work with.

Many editing programmes will generate their own file types, depending on the type of footage you are importing, but also allow you to import and edit other supported files. Common file types such as QuickTime's .MOV and Microsoft's .AVI are widely used for editing and are supported by numerous systems. They allow you to use a choice of codecs for different purposes. So for instance, you could create two QuickTime .MOV versions of your finished film, but one would use a codec for Internet streaming, while another might be for creating a DVD version of your film. The most important aspect of working with files is that you choose a file type that will maintain the resolution of the footage you started with and that is supported by other programmes you might need to use in your workflow.

Edit decision list (EDL)

An EDL is a series of time code numbers that relate to both your master source footage and the times and events that you have created during an edit.

EDLs are used to recreate versions of an offline edit for an online edit or auto conform, as well as for grading of the takes that will be used. Most editing systems are capable of generating them, and because they relate to

Figure 47.
Example of an EDL giving precise times for all edit points.

213

the original source material, they can be read by other editing systems, or people such as editors or neg cutters, who then use the information to create the online.

Auto conform

An auto conform or conform edit is the process of reassembling the master version of the film based on the EDL.

Rendering

Most editing systems allow you to work with virtual versions of your master footage. Small compressed files are used for speed and efficiency instead of the full-resolution larger files. Any effects such as transitions that you apply to the virtual timeline version need to be created with the original files. This takes longer than with the virtual versions, resulting in the processing times involved in rendering.

Digitising

Digitising is the process of converting analogue information into digital. This used to be a time-consuming process with many early digital editing systems, where analogue video had to be captured and digitised. Now that video formats are predominantly digital, this is not as much of an issue, with many transfers directly from cameras or VTR decks using a digital transfer such as firewire, where no digitising is required. Many capture cards for analogue sources still provide digitising, but, due to processing speeds, this can often occur in real time.

Storage

Working on NLE editing systems, the amount of information and the speed with which you can work with it will be two of your major concerns; these factors are not governed by the software you are using, but by the computer it is running on. The speed of the computer processor and the amount of RAM will determine how quickly the computer can process the type of files you are working with. The amount of footage you can store on the computer will be governed by the hard disc space available. Computer storage used to be slow and expensive, but firewire hard drives are quick and efficient means of storing and retrieving footage for your film. Depending on the format and resolution of the files you are using it is practical and fairly cheap to store several hours worth of rushes on a single hard drive, or array of hard drives.

Backing up

One of the most important considerations when working with digital files of your film is backing everything up. Keeping at least two digital versions of your rushes on separate external hard drives is really a must. As stable as most computer systems are these days there is still the potential for things to go wrong and work to be lost. Backing your progress up to external hard drives allows you an element of security if everything goes haywire.

Titles and credits

Final Cut Pro and Adobe Premiere both have the ability to create high-resolution titles and credits for your film, which can be outputted to the final version. For anything beyond the ability offered by these programmes there are a whole host of other programmes that can be used to create titles and credits, from Adobe After Effects to plain old Photoshop. The most important consideration when using other programmes outside of your editing software is that the file formats and resolutions are, or can be, matched to your film.

Digital effects

Just as digital software has put editing into the hands of most people with a computer, it has also allowed amazingly sophisticated effects and compositing programmes to become domesticated. Whereas outside of Hollywood computer-generated effects for films (CGI) used to look really rubbish, these days you can easily purchase state of the art software programmes that are the same as the ones used on massive-budget feature films. Adobe After Effects or Apple's Shake are regularly used on multi-million-dollar Hollywood films, yet for often a few hundred pounds can be purchased off the shelf and quite happily used on a reasonably powerful home computer. Learning how to use them or finding someone who does is really the only thing that will stop you from being able to generate realistic digital effects.

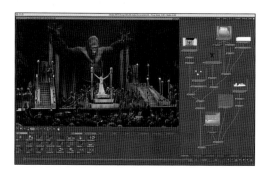

Figure 48.
Apple's *Shake* compositing programme.

Locking the edit

Once you have fine-tuned your edit then you need to lock the film off. This means that you lock the timeline and video tracks so that the clips cannot be moved. This is important as it allows sound designers and composers to work on the film potentially using the time code and clip lengths as a guide. If they are working with an unlocked edit they might complete their work to find that you've changed the durations meaning that they then have to recompose.

SOUND EDITING

Mixing and editing the three components of your soundtrack (effects, score and dialogue) can be performed either within the editing programme or in dedicated programmes designed specifically for soundtrack composition or editing.

Final Cut Pro and Premiere offer extensive audio editing that allows you to run large amounts (often up to 100) tracks of audio simultaneously. Working on the same principle as editing your footage, you can create complex compositions of audio by working on the individual tracks in turn, using time code or visual references to sync the score, dialogue and effects with the film.

Sound editing, although an intricate process, can often be performed by whoever is cutting the film. When working with a composer or sound designer, who is working on a dedicated music programme, it is easy enough to choose a digital format that can be shared between the programmes. Just like video clips and files, there are also dedicated audio files. The most ubiquitous of these are WAV and AIFF file types. These are again container files, and so different codecs can be used to encode the audio data. Because audio files generally contain much less information than video files, there is often no need for them to be compressed, allowing any transfers required for composing and editing to occur at full quality, whether on a CD or sent over the Internet.

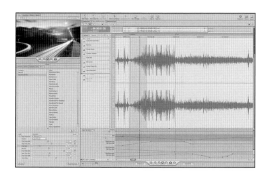

Figure 49.
Soundtrack Pro by Apple works in tandem with *Final Cut Pro*.

Sound mixing

Although sound syncing and editing can often be performed by an editor, sound mixing is a much more complex task. Once all the elements of your soundtrack are in place, a mix is performed to adjust both the volume and the frequencies of the individual tracks that make up the whole soundtrack.

Although most editing programmes will allow you to perform this function, even offering effects such as reverb and equalisation, creating a professional mix really requires somebody with talent and experience. The most obvious element of sound mixing is adjusting the volumes of the individual tracks, allowing the most important elements to be clear and audible. The second and much more complicated role of the sound mixer is equalisation, whereby the soundtrack is adjusted so that different elements such as voices or instruments each inhabit their own frequency range. A basic mix will separate types of sound and the emphasis required for them into different ranges. Steps in frequency between bass, middle and treble are used so that the final mix allows all the different elements to coexist within a dynamic range, giving your soundtrack a finesse and depth that it might otherwise lack. Depending on how complex your soundtrack is and the production values of your whole film, a professional sound mixer may or may not be required. If you can't get a sound mixer and you feel you need one, it's worth looking into programmes like Soundtrack Pro from Final Cut studio, which offers soundtrack analysis programmes that will auto perform basic but effective mixes of your finished soundtrack.

26. SOUNDTRACK

With so much of your attention focused on the visual side of the filmmaking process, it's often easy to forget the importance of the soundtrack. Without the extra dimension of sound, your film would lose a lot of its potential impact. Even though we often take it for granted when watching films, it is amazing how much the use of sound adds to our viewing experience and our ability to absorb the images. Even the subtlest of sounds when added to an image has the potential to bring it alive and give the audience the focus that you are intending. The soundtrack has the potential to draw the viewer into your film on a subconscious level and amplify the action that is taking place. The same piece of film, when seen with different pieces of music, or even ambient sound, can come across very differently, and the mood can change dramatically even though the footage remains exactly the same.

This is why organising the time to give the soundtrack the importance it deserves will pay dividends when it comes to creating your film. Whether you are intending just to use your location and dialogue recordings or are planning on a fully orchestrated score, it is an important element to start planning early in the film's pre-production.

DIALOGUE

This consists of recordings of the dialogue from your script. It is often recorded on set when you are filming (see sound recording section). It can also be recorded in a studio at a later date and then synced to the film. This process is known as Automatic Dialogue Replacement (ADR). Any narration in your film is normally recorded afterwards in this way too. Although ADR recordings are generally better quality it can be a complicated and time-consuming process to synchronise ADR with footage of actors already delivering those lines. So ensuring that the sound quality of your location recordings is as good as possible is essential.

SOUND EFFECTS

The sound effect section of the audio is often made up of a combination of both location sounds, recorded at the time of filming, and additional sounds that are either created by a foley artist, or sourced from a sound effects library. Location sound recordings alone often don't have the necessary impact, so the sound of a door slamming, an engine starting or a gun firing are often replaced with the relevant effect afterwards. On feature films, it's the foley artist's job to create ultra-realistic sound effects, normally from unrelated objects, and recreate bespoke sound effects: the sound of a bird's wings flapping made with rubber gloves, for example. On a short film, the budget would rarely allow for the hire of a foley artist to create sound effects. However, there are lots of online sound libraries where you can acquire either foley artist effects or extremely high-quality live recordings. Larger sound library websites allow you to audition multiple options for even the most random of

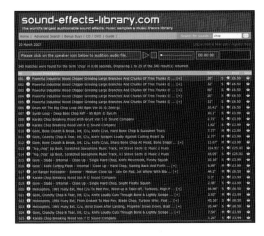

Figure 50.
Sound effects library
downloadable file options.

sounds. Once you have selected the right one it can be downloaded directly as a high-quality sound file for a fee. The files are in formats supported by most editing programmes so they can be imported straight onto an audio track and mixed into the rest of the soundtrack.

http://www.sound-effects-library.com
http://www.f7sound.com

Sound design

Sound design is the creation of ambient or atmospherics for a film. Unlike a music score, sound design doesn't involve classic composition techniques, but relies more on layering textures of sound to create a mood or tone. Sound designers often work closely with composers so that the score and sound design complement and extend the same moods and themes of the film.

MUSIC

Traditionally films have an original score created by a composer. This score is then played by musicians and recorded, then synchronised to the film. The number of musicians involved can range from a huge orchestra to a lone music programmer.

Whatever the style of music, film scores generally contain a central theme or melody. This then reoccurs throughout and gives coherence to the soundtrack as a whole. This use of musical themes is sometimes broken down further so that each of the main characters – protagonist/antagonist – has their own accompanying theme or leitmotif.

There is no orthodox method for creating short film scores and there are as many approaches to soundtrack composition as there are styles of music. Whether you want classical, songs by a band or ambient textures, the one thing that you should avoid is using music that has already been commercially released because it will be subject to publishing, broadcasting and synchronisation rights and need clearance to be used in a film. Unfortunately licensing music is an expensive and complicated procedure that would generally far exceed the budgets of most short films. As tempting as it may be to even use only a small snippet of unlicensed music in your film, the result may well be that your film will not be accepted at festivals and will not be eligible for broadcast. If you are adamant that you want to license and clear a piece of music then you can find more information at the following sites.

http://www.ascap.com
http://www.mcps.co.uk

The exception to this rule is music that is now public domain. This means pieces of music that are over 50 years old. Recordings of these pieces are still liable to royalties and publishing rights, but you can legally record a version of them. See the following sites for more information.

http://www.pdinfo.com
http://www.royaltyfreemusic.com

There are also audio or sound libraries that stock thousands of pieces of pre-recorded music, for which, as with sound effects, you can pay a flat fee, giving you exclusive rights to use the music in your film.

Original score

Generally the most interesting option is to have a composer or sound designer create an original score for your film. There are a huge amount of composers and musicians that are looking for opportunities to compose film soundtracks. The challenge is to find someone that will create a soundtrack that will complement the atmosphere and mood of your film.

INTERVIEW WITH RACHEL HAMILTON (COMPOSER)

Rachel Hamilton is a classically trained musician and multi-instrumentalist with a passion for old synthesisers, Theremins and harps. She has composed original soundtracks for over 20 short films as well as recording solo projects. Further information can be found at www.rachelhamilton.com.

At what stage of the short filmmaking process does the director or producer normally get in touch with you and is there an ideal time?

Usually they get in touch when the film is almost ready for music, but I've had one occasion when I was onboard even before the script was written, and the scriptwriter/director had some of my pre-written music playing while she wrote! Ideally I'd like to be signed up with a bit of notice so I can keep that time aside in my diary if it looks like a good project. But I don't want to be writing music for a film that gets re-edited beyond recognition, so when the film is getting into shape and nearing its last stages of editing is good.

How do you normally go about working with a director while composing for their film?

Generally we watch the edited film together for the first time, then talk about ideas, watch it again and discuss what kind of music needs to go where, and swap ideas. Then I go away and write some music, and we talk about what I've done, what needs changing, what doesn't work, what does work. And so on until it's ready. This can be done in person, or over the phone or by email. I've done a lot of work with comments bouncing back over email.

Do you find it easier or more difficult if the director gives you a lot of input and is more exacting about what they want?

Generally this is really helpful; it can be inspiring to work with constrictions, and if ideas spark more ideas that's great. Composers are meant to hate temp scores but they can be helpful too, especially if time is very tight. A director who doesn't have a clue what he wants could mean a wonderful blank canvas for the composer, or it could be he's indecisive and doesn't like anything.

How do you go about the process of beginning to write the score for a short film?

223

Do you just start at the beginning and finish at the end?

No, rarely. Maybe there's one bit I'm itching to write some music for, or something comes to me straight away, so I just start with whatever is ready to be written in my mind. Once the score is started it opens my mind up to what might happen in the rest of the score. It's a tense period when I've written the first bit and I'm waiting to hear from the director if it's what he or she wants. I don't want to write an entire score and have to start again.

Technically, how should the filmmaker present their film to you for you to begin creating the soundtrack?

A DVD or video is great to get started on, so I can see the full picture on a decent sized screen, but when it comes to the final cut I like working with a small-ish QuickTime file as this is really easy to synch with my music software.

Technically, how do you then fit the film with the music, what programme do you use for this and what does the recording process entail?

I use Digital Performer, a Mac only sequencer/audio package. I usually begin by recording ideas in midi (rather than recorded audio) so I can move them around, change the speed, cut and copy. Digital Performer is very good at finding a tempo to synch hit points with the music successfully. I don't use hard synch as often as I used to, but it's a useful tool to have on my sequencer.

What happens once you have done something that you think works well? Do you then go back to the director and see what he thinks?

Yes, I try to do a good mock up with samples, but don't spend too much time shaping the sounds and recording live instruments. I might be inadvertently on the wrong track altogether, so it's better to get it to him quickly but well enough recorded that he can hear what the music is about.

Is it now possible to simulate a huge orchestral score on computers and synthesisers?

It is, but it's pretty painstaking to make it sound half reasonable. Even with the best samples it takes time to go through all 20 or so violin sections to see which sounds best, then to add in realistic fades, swells... It might fool most of the people some of the time, not all the people all the time. To my ears string sections can be OK, but sampled solo strings or woodwind are really bland. I prefer to work with a small selection of real instruments. It has more oomph;

samples sound compressed and dull and lack the little glitches and the soul of real instrumentalists.

Once you have finished the soundtrack on what format do you give it to the film-maker? Does it then need mixing or is it ready to be put on the film and shown?

Quite often I'll email an mp3 whilst writing, or put it on a CD as audio. For the final music I'll provide an audio CD (stereo) unless the director has specifically requested AIFFs, which can be at 44.1 or 48 MHz. I do my own mixing, some-times providing a more bass-heavy option for the filmmaker to choose between, and the sound editor might tweak the EQ or add a bit more reverb. For higher-budget productions I may have to one day provide music as separate tracks, which could be 8 tracks ADAT or Pro-Tools. I haven't had this requested as yet.

What are the commonest problems you encounter when trying to score a film?

Getting started can be tricky sometimes. I've found coffee and pastries to be one of the very best ways to get me buzzing with ideas. Also deadlines. And, most importantly, good films. Lack of time can be a problem. The biggest prob-lem has probably been finding good musicians who are prepared to record for little in return, or a recommended musician who it turns out can't read music or who can't play in tune. When I have a tight deadline and the recording is going painfully slowly or not at all that's a real low point.

What can the filmmaker do to make your life as easy as possible when it comes to you creating a soundtrack for their film?

Provide coffee and pastries.

Make a good film, give me a reasonable amount of time to score it, provide me with an easy format to work from, keep me up to date on edit changes (please not too many!), give me constructive feedback on what I've written so far and be inspiring to be around.

Is it now possible to create a score by just sending emails and mp3s back and forth between the composer and the director? Have you ever worked in this way?

Yes, I've worked with directors in the US and the UK this way. In a couple of instances we've never even spoken on the phone, but sent lots of emails, and built up a good understanding. Sometimes having things clearly written is ever so useful; I can re-read it if I'm not sure what they were getting at first, or re-mind myself when I need some inspiration.

Do you ever get asked to play from sheet music a composition that is now public domain?

I've done some arranging of traditional music, which is fine, but not had to just play from a score. I'm a composer not a performer – okay, I am a performer, but only of my own music – so it wouldn't be my thing to play someone else's music. Rearranging someone else's ideas could be a creative exercise if the music was to be shaped and varied to flow with the film, and co-composing can be rewarding.

What advice do you have when it comes to short film directors looking for composers? Where is a good place to start?

Recommendation is the best way, or if you admire a score you've heard and seen, maybe at a film festival, try getting in touch with the composer. Shooting People is a good source; though even the dreariest films solicit up to 100 CDs from potential composers and you'll have to listen to a lot of inappropriate submissions before finding someone possible. You can search for composers on Shooting People and visit their websites, probably less time-consuming. My website is a great place to start!

How long does it normally take you from receiving the film to completing the finished soundtrack?

I've had a weekend to score a short at one extreme, three or four months being about the longest. Usually it's a month or two. In a way, a shortish deadline gets me focused. If there's no end date I could put it on the back-burner for too long and miss out on the ideas-generating buzz when I start working on a new film.

What do you enjoy most about composing for short films?

I get really excited when a new DVD pops through the post, or watching it for the first time and discussing all the possibilities with the director. The very best bit is probably when I'm on a roll and the music seems to be composing itself, which does generally happen after staring at a blank keyboard for long enough.

27. FILM TRANSFER

TELECINE (TK)

Telecine or TK is a process for transferring film onto a video format. The term is also used to refer to the equipment involved in the process.

Telecine is conventionally used to transfer an exposed and developed 16mm or 35mm negative onto a digital or analogue tape format. This allows the film to be viewed on video, without having to make a print of the negative. It can be used to transfer film onto multiple formats, often simultaneously, which means that having a negative telecined once can produce a VHS viewing copy for immediately watching the rushes, a low-resolution copy such as MiniDV for offline editing and a master copy for online editing.

The equipment used to perform a telecine projects a beam through the negative, which is then transformed into an electronic signal. This can be outputted to nearly any video format by the required recording deck being linked to the machine.

Telecine scans the negative in real time and at the same frame rate that the film was shot at. Telecine systems vary in quality, and the resolution of image they produce is dependent on both the quality of the machine and the format you are recording out to. Conventional telecine systems work at resolutions of up to 2K (see resolution) but this then needs to be recorded to a format that can capture this resolution. Telecine is now surpassed in quality by Digital Intermediate systems that use a different type of scanning process, which is purely digital.

When do you telecine?

Telecine is carried out after the negative has been developed, often at the same facility that has developed the negative. This is often done overnight, so that rushes can be dropped off in the evening and viewed in the morning.

This allows the rushes to be watched on video, rather than a print having to be made and projected. The telecine is often outputted to several formats at the same time, for different purposes, such as analogue or digital versions of the rushes for offline or online editing.

When the telecine takes place, time code is recorded onto the video format which refers directly to the frame numbers of the film stock and starts with the first frame of the negative which has a hole punched through it. This is essential, so that any offline editing will still produce an EDL that will refer to the frames of the negative, allowing neg cuts and further scans to be performed accurately.

Types of telecine

The quality of telecine you need will depend on the formats you are using for your post-production workflow. Depending on what you are using your telecine video versions for there are several different types of telecine you can have done.

One light
A one light telecine is a transfer where the first shot on a roll of negative is given a neutral balance in brightness, contrast and colour, and the entire rushes are then transferred with these settings.

Best light
This is a telecine where each shot is stopped and brightness, contrast and colour settings are set for each, until the entire rushes are transferred.

Full grade
A full grade can be performed at any time the neg is going through a telecine,

but unless this is the final transfer then it is normally not necessary (see grading).

Other options that are offered at the telecine stage are choices over aspect ratio, letterboxing and burnt-in time code.

DIGITAL INTERMEDIATE (DI)

Digital Intermediate is widely used to refer to a film transfer and workflow that is purely digital. This is a relatively new workflow for film, but is becoming increasingly popular. The technology was first used on an entire feature film in 2000, but since then this type of workflow has become ubiquitous for high-end film productions of any length.

Operating at higher resolutions than telecine systems, digital laser scanners are used to scan the negative film frame by frame; this method allows huge amounts of information from the original negative to be stored. This information is then stored as digital files on computer hard drives or other storage devices. This digital version is then the master version and the film negative is not used anymore; any subsequent film print versions are made from the digital master not the original negative.

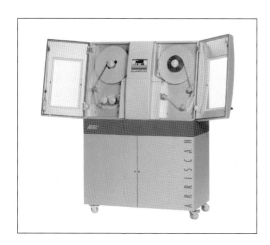

Figure 51.
Arri laser scanning produces
digital files of each frame.

Why DI?

The advantage of DI is that the entire post-production of the film can take place on one format, with no need for offline editing, neg cuts and shifting between formats.

The entire film can be edited, graded and have effects added digitally on computer-based systems allowing the entire post-production workflow to take place at full quality. Because of this the finished film can then be transferred back out to a film print without any loss of quality, which could not be achieved with a telecine.

Extremely appealing as a potential workflow for a film, for short filmmakers this has several drawbacks. Being a new technology, DI is very in demand and therefore not a cheap workflow. The other disadvantage of DI for short films is the high quality itself. Currently S16 is scanned at 2K (see resolution) and 35mm at 4K. This creates two dilemmas. First, each single frame of the film as a single digital file can be very sizable, so an entire film's rushes requires lots of dedicated hard drive storage, which is expensive. Second, once you've got this amount of digital film information on hard drives you need a computer that can play it back and potentially manipulate it. This requires a very powerful computer designed specifically with this purpose in mind.

That said, DI is still an option for short filmmakers with the right budget; prices are falling constantly and there are now top-range prosumer computers that are capable of handling this amount of information.

28. GRADING

Grading is also known as colour timing or colour correction. It is a process that alters the appearance of a video or film image by adjusting the colour palette, brightness and contrast. It is an optional process that is normally performed in the final stages of post-production and provided by post-production facilities.

Grading can be performed on either film or video images, and you will have seen examples of it in feature films, commercials and music videos, all of which will have been through this process in post-production.

The purpose of grading is to manipulate the raw footage, by emphasising or subduing hues and tones so as to give a certain scene or entire film an overall look. It can be used in several ways:

- To bring the film closer to how it appeared to you at the time of shooting, rather than how it appears once recorded on a format, thus giving it a more realistic look.
- To visually emphasise atmospheres by enhancing certain colours, brightness and contrast. It therefore allows you to match the visual style with the mood of a scene or the film and create a unique look.
- To rectify discrepancies in colour and exposure that might occur while shooting, allowing you to match shots that might initially look different.

Why grade your film?

Although grading is technically a fine-tuning process for the look of your film, it is not one that should be overlooked.

However good a job you or your DP has done while shooting your film, the chances are that, due to idiosyncrasies that occur when using lighting, cameras and stock, your film may look very different than you thought it would. Many film or video 'looks' cannot be achieved while shooting. However much time and effort you put into lighting and choosing a format, they have limited abilities to create the type of looks that you can achieve with a grading process.

Yet another way to control the image, it is a tool that can be used subliminally to help tell a story and create a professional-looking film. Not merely a finishing touch, used creatively it's a process that can have a huge impact on your film.

Grading of both film and video can be performed in a variety of ways and at different stages. This is normally performed by a colourist or grader who relies on their experience and talent to perform the technical processes.

GRADING FILM

Film, both 35mm and S16mm, due to its high resolution and dynamic range, is ideal for grading. Traditionally, film grading was performed as a photo-chemical process, whereby a negative was processed in a laboratory with a Hazeltine system. The Hazeltine employed a series of techniques to subdue certain colour ranges or boost others and even removed certain chemical elements from the negative.

Many feature films still make use of these techniques, however, and over the last decade more and more films have been transferred onto a digital format, either through telecine or Digital Intermediate stages, then graded using digital technology. Dedicated suites that use a combination of software and hardware can be used to grade film negatives as they are being transferred onto a digital format such as tape or a hard drive.

GRADING VIDEO

Video, unlike film, is often already in the digital realm, so can be graded using much of the same computer-based systems that are used for grading film without the need for telecine or scanning.

Figure 52. Da Vinci Grading Suite.

However, because most video formats have much less colour space (see video formats) than film, the type of video format you shoot your film on will determine to what extent it can be graded. DV footage contains very minimal colour space, so there is not much information to work with in the first place, whereas HD formats contain much better colour space information and are much more feasible for colour correction.

DIGITAL GRADING

Contemporary digital grading systems are amazingly powerful tools. The amount of creative and corrective control that can be achieved with them is far beyond what could be done with traditional photochemical processes. Digital grading systems vary in their capabilities, with older systems being more limited. At the high end of grading systems, it is now possible to control not just the hue and saturation or brightness and contrast of the whole image, but also break an image into different zones, each of which can be graded separately. For instance, the leaves on a tree can be processed differently to the colour of the sky or the skin tone of a face.

PROFESSIONAL GRADING

Professional grading, like most post-production stages, is generally charged by the hour and it can be very expensive. When you get a film graded, you are not just paying for the use of the facilities; you are also paying for the skill and expertise of the grader. Grading, due to its improving capabilities, is increasingly a creative process. It's not only something that requires technical ability, but also talent.

When considering where to get a grade for your film done, you not only have to weigh up the quality of the facilities but also the skill of the person who will be grading it.

DIY GRADING

With the increased quality of video formats, processors and software, it is now both possible and cost-effective to carry out grading on domestic computers.

Software editing packages such as Final Cut Pro and Adobe Premiere offer extensive and sophisticated colour correction tools that can be used to carry out fairly sophisticated colour correction. Capitalising on the higher resolution and dynamic range of HD formats, there are now starting to be software packages that offer dedicated programmes purely for grading.

With just a few hours of grading at a post-production house often costing as much as the entire budget of many short films, using this type of software is often the only possibility many shorts will have to be graded.

The disadvantages of this home grading solution is that, even with the increased abilities of programmes such as Adobe After Effects or specialist systems like Final Touch, grading is still a process that takes a lot of technical skill and experience.

Just to become competent and have an all-round knowledge of grading is a long process. Using this technical know-how creatively then takes experience and practice. One of the most feasible solutions to this dilemma is a programme called Magic Bullet Editors by Red Giant software. Working from within both Premiere and Final Cut Pro, this programme allows you to select from a huge variety of preset grades, giving you the option to choose from very sophisticated film looks. The programme even offers film damage effects and other film-like filters that can be applied to video.

http://www.redgiantsoftware.com/mbforeditors.html

Budget saving

There are several ways to try getting a cheap grade for your film. Try and find assistant graders who are looking to practice their skills and ask at post houses if they have anyone who might be interested in your project. These assistants may not yet be the best in the industry, but will often have a lot of technical experience, access to facilities and potential talent.

Try and use older systems to grade on; the high end is more expensive.

When do you grade?

Full grading is often the finishing touch undertaken as a final step before the film goes onto the screening format.

With video formats grading is left until the edit has been locked and the film is otherwise complete. After all there is no point in grading shots that won't make it into the final cut. Grading can be time-consuming, so you don't want to grade any more footage than you really need.

When a film has been shot on either S16 or 35mm the film will often be transferred from the negative twice. An initial telecine, to transfer the film to a video format for creating an offline edit, will not be graded as such as this footage is merely for creating an offline EDL.

Once the film has been edited offline, then the EDL is used to telecine or scan the relevant parts of the negative, and at this stage they will go through a full grade, so that you eliminate the need to grade all of the footage, and can concentrate on the parts you know are going into your finished film.

29. MASTER AND SCREENING FORMATS

Apart from choosing a format to shoot your film on you need to choose a format or formats to master and screen your film on.

Having completed a finished version of your film, you then need to output it, producing a master version of your film that all subsequent copies are made from. This should be at the highest quality warranted by the resolution at which you have completed the rest of your workflow. It's common practice to create a master copy on several different formats for different duplication and screening options. Most transfer and post-production houses will allow you to master your film to a single format and then make duplicate versions onto other formats. As a general rule, the prices both for the actual media (such as tapes) and the actual transfer costs are generally reflected in the quality they provide.

35mm print

Creating a 35mm screening print is the ideal for exhibition screening in cinemas and film festivals. Classic film printing from 35mm negatives or S16 blow ups offers incredible quality. New laser-scanning technology now also allows transfers from low or high-resolution video formats from MiniDV to HD-cam, which also produces outstanding results. The drawback to this quality is the expense. Creating a film print from a negative is costly but transferring from video is even more expensive. Video to film prices vary depending on the technology and quality involved; they generally average at about £1,000 per minute. Some international film festivals will only accept films from 35mm prints.

Figure 53.
35mm screening print.
Incredible quality but very expensive.

HDCAM-SR, HDCAM D5 and HDCAM

HD formats provide incredible quality for creating a master copy of your film that can then be used to create film prints or lower-resolution copies. Although HD formats are superb quality there isn't really much point in having your film transferred to one of these formats unless it's been created at HD resolution. HD formats are still not standard for film festivals and only some broadcast. Soon this will all change and HD tapes will be the screening formats of choice, but for the moment it is still DigiBeta.

Figure 54.
HDCAM tape stock.
High resolution but not currently accepted by many film festivals.

Digital Betacam/DigiBeta and Betacam SP

DigiBeta is generally the short film standard master and screening format, and most broadcast and film festivals will require a DigiBeta screening version of your film. Although standard resolution, it is a very high-quality and stable format. Beta SP is the analogue equivalent, and is also screened at many festivals. Both NTSC and PAL versions need to be produced if you are intending to distribute your film internationally.

Figure 55.
Digital betacam.
Standard format for
most broadcasters and
film festivals.

MiniDV

Although some festivals will screen MiniDV tapes, the fragile nature of the format is not ideal for either mastering or screening.

DVD/VHS

Most film festivals don't actually screen DVD copies of short films. However, they are often required as preview copies to send to festivals for the selection process. They are also essential formats to have multiple copies of your film on, as they are ideal for promoting your film, being far cheaper and less cumbersome to send out than the screening copies.

30. DISTRIBUTION

FESTIVALS

Film festivals provide short filmmakers with an ideal platform to bring their films to audiences around the world. They potentially give you the chance not only to showcase your film, but also to meet other like-minded filmmakers and promote your film to distributors and backers.

There are literally thousands of film festivals that run annual screenings. They range from huge international film industry showcases, down to small independent festivals.

There are several important factors that differentiate types of film festivals from each other. The first and most obvious is that not all film festivals are short film festivals; some are just film festivals geared towards screening feature films, but will also run a short film programme. The others are short film festivals that exclusively show short films.

Even given this simple division, there is still a huge amount of short film festivals, some of which specialise further in a type or genre of short film, such as comedy or experimental; others cater for all kinds of short films but have different programmes for different categories of film.

Some of these festivals run each programme as a competition with awards and cash prizes, while others are non-competitive.

The common factor between all these festivals is that, competitive or not, they all have a selection process through which your film will have to go. Only if it's selected will it be shown.

Given that there is so much variety when it comes to film festivals, the best approach is to develop a list of film festivals that you want to target. To do this, it's a good idea to have a look at your motivation for making the film in the first place. If you have made a short film with the purpose of trying to promote yourself as a writer/director, and are aiming to one day direct a feature film, then you are going to need a very different strategy to someone who has made a short simply to exercise some creative freedom and experiment with the medium of film.

You should research as many festivals as you can and try and work out which festivals would suit your film. Different festivals will give you access to different audiences, and they will also have very different selection criteria. Which type of festivals you decide to enter should be decided on the grounds of which type of audiences you want your film to be seen by. Ideally you should target festivals that are both likely to cater for a film such as yours and to have a selection process that will mean it is likely to be screened.

Many film festivals charge a submission fee, which covers the administrative costs of dealing with your submission and does not lead to profit on their part, but only spend the money if you think it is worthwhile and your film has a legitimate chance of being selected.

Aiming for high-calibre festivals such as Cannes or Raindance may seem like the fastest route to a large audience, but there are factors that you should bear in mind. Most large-scale festivals will be aimed, primarily, at promoting feature films, and are normally industry and sponsorship funded. They will, however, often have a short film section, for which there will generally be a fee for submission. The fee will be non-refundable and will get your film into the selection process. This does not mean your film will necessarily be selected. Larger festivals will often only screen films that have a 35mm print (see formats). If your film is not on 35mm then transfer can be extremely expensive. If you have been planning for this since the early stages of your film then the large international festivals can be the ideal arenas for your film. However, you should also consider the fact that short films at these festivals are often given second place to features, so don't always get the attention you might hope for.

There are a growing number of festivals dedicated solely to short films. They range from very established international festivals such as Clermont Ferrand or Oberhausen to regional independent festivals such as Halloween or Brief Encounters. Large international short film festivals are often designed to partly function as a showcase for the television and distribution industries, with many of them running a film market for distributors and buyers parallel to the festival itself. If you are aiming to sell your film, or have it distributed by a company, then these festivals are geared towards helping filmmakers promote their films to prospective buyers, and are a great place to network and meet other filmmakers, as well as watch a lot of other films from around the world. They also offer awards, which, if you are lucky enough to win, will help raise your film's profile.

The smaller-scale short film festivals are also ideal places to show your film and view other filmmakers'. They are generally organised and run by people that are passionate about short films, and don't have the pressure of commercial backing. They are great places to see up and coming filmmakers' shorts, and are worth attending whether you have a film to show or not. The smaller festivals generally have more of a filmmaking community atmosphere and excitement about them, and for many filmmakers there it will be the first experience of watching their film on the big screen. They also offer you the chance to meet people who have probably been through similar experiences in getting their short made.

Not only will these festivals be orientated towards short films, they often have screening and selection programmes that are divided into more specific genres. Rather than just submit your film into an eclectic short film section, you can enter it into a specific genre that fits your film's profile. Not only will your film be screened in the relevant genre, it will also be judged for selection or awards based on the merits of how it performs within the genre. So, for example, if it is a comedy, it will be judged against other comedies rather than against a horror or experimental film.

With over 3,000 film festivals taking place round the world every year, it may be a good idea to start out by submitting to a local regional festival first, then work outwards from there. Festival organisers generally attend as many other film events as they can, so you will often be invited to submit to other festivals by organisers who have seen your film at another event.

INTERVIEW WITH PHILIP ILSON (FESTIVAL ORGANISER)

With roots going back to 1994, Halloween Short Film Festival has been running since 2004. Set up and run by Philip Ilson and Kate Taylor, Halloween has rapidly become one of the most cutting edge short film festivals in the UK.

What led you to set up a short film festival?

Halloween had been running as a screening organisation for short film since 1994 – and there's a 'history' on our website at www.shortfilms.org.uk – but to sum up, we initially started screening short films above pubs after being inspired by Exploding Cinema shows. There were few other screening opportunities for shorts in the mid 90s, so in the wake of us and Exploding starting out, a few other film clubs sprang up and in 1995/6 we collaborated on an underground film festival called Volcano. Although Halloween held monthly screenings for five years, mainly at Notre Dame Hall off Leicester Square, we began to branch out into multi-media and music events which included Kentra in London, Sensurround, which was a touring event for the British Council, and then, in about 2001, Full Length at the ICA, which was where live bands performed new soundtracks to feature films. In the early 90s we kind of dropped out of regular shorts screenings mainly because there were so many; with audiences being spread out, they were going down. With the amount of screenings there was an element of overkill. Also, short filmmakers weren't getting anything special by getting a screening in a bar in, say, Peckham.

But looking at the climate in 2003 with all these screenings, there were no film festivals purely dedicated to shorts outside of Brief Encounters in Bristol and Kinofilm in Manchester; certainly nothing in London. Of course, shorts screened in festivals, but always as a sidebar. As we had ICA support with the Full Length events, we put in a proposal to them to set up a short film festival, but in using the ICA we could have the Halloween multi-media stamp by using the live music area and bar, as well as two cinemas for screenings, which is something we hadn't really done before – show films in a cinema!

How do you see Halloween in the context of other film festivals that screen shorts?

Halloween has a 'brand' that we hope is a bit more edgy and away from the industry; we're not interested in Cannes or Soho House, but look for quirky leftfield or lower-budget work. Not to say we won't screen the big stuff – John Williams' *Hibernation* won an award at this year's festival, to add to his cupboard-full of awards from around the world. We also championed Andrea Arnold from her first film and held a retrospective of her work on the eve of her Oscar triumph, and now she's up for a Palme d'Or in Cannes for her first feature. But we like to champion work that may not get screenings at more mainstream industry-led festivals, and it's good to mix these varying types of films within the themed programmes that we curate.

Also, this year, we had a music documentary shorts strand – because this is something that no other festival has done, we've toured the package around the UK and it's also played in Berlin and Amsterdam.

In the years since Halloween started, have you noticed an improvement in the visual quality of the films that you have screened?

Not really. Some of my favourite short films are those from when we first started screening shorts in the mid 90s – Andrew Kotting, Jamie Thraves, Alison Murray, Vito Rocco. In many ways, the quality of ideas is worse, as there's an element of 'anyone can do it', so there's an excess of bad films. Not to say the gems and masterpieces aren't out there. Also, on a purely technical front, we don't look for technically brilliant filmmaking, but for ideas. This is echoed in competitions like DepicT!

What do you look for when selecting short films for the festival?

Good question, but impossible to answer. The selection process is purely a personal taste issue. I think we're quite harsh at Halloween, but there's only two of us and each year more films come in. Harsh, but fair... I like it when a programme comes together and it's like your baby that you're proud of. You're excited about people coming and watching the films and discovering them for the first time, echoing the feeling you get when you first see them.

What are the benefits for filmmakers of showing their film at festivals?

Screening in a festival has better kudos than in an obscure bar, and I hope that doesn't sound too snobbish – after all Halloween came from these bars in the first place. Also, Halloween doesn't care about films having previous screenings, like many festivals do. Something like *Hibernation* must have screened in every venue in London before we screened it, and it still won an award. What slightly annoys me is that filmmakers on their CVs mention the venue over Halloween. As we use the prestigious ICA and Curzon cinemas, the ICA Short Film Festival or the Curzon Short Film Festival sounds more impressive than the Halloween Short Film Festival. But hopefully we can build up a brand.

What kind of audience do you get attending the festival?

The unfortunate answer is 'friends and family' – by default, the main audience at a short film screening are those connected with the films on the screen. Annoyingly, whole waves of people crowd out of cinemas after their film has shown, which is really disrespectful to other filmmakers who have their work on. But it happens. We try and make our short film programme themes of interest to a general audience though, and our horror and Fortean programmes usually sell out on theme name alone. Also, Halloween has all these other elements, such as the live music and bar visuals events, so we always make sure performers tell audiences that they're here as part of a film festival.

Have you seen a rise in the number of people attending film festivals?

Yes, the audiences are bigger due to their being more films and filmmakers. But there's still that element of saturation point, I'm sure. Short films or short film screenings also go through 'trendy' periods, where the media picks up on them, which means a more general audience attends. Our Kentra nights back in the late 90s were featured in *The Face* and *Dazed & Confused* etc, so that whole 'cool' thing meant more people wanted to be part of it. This still continues with 'brands' like onedotzero, and we do hope the Halloween brand continues to make people want to attend regardless.

Have you seen short film directors that have shown at Halloween go on to direct features?

Yes, many. Although, unfortunately, very few have done it successfully. Promising names like Jamie Thraves, who made some great late 1990s' shorts and got a name as a promo director for people like Radiohead, disappeared without a trace after his first feature *The Lowdown*. We did screen Guy Ritchie's first short in the early days...

One director we've been championing since Halloween started is Andrew Kotting, and he still continues to make excellent work in a variety of art forms (we're working with him again on an arts project). Another Halloween fave Alison Murray has made a superb debut feature *Mouth to Mouth*, but she's been having trouble finding a UK distributor. Bizarrely, we showed a short film by Scottish filmmaker Jim Gillespie who hotfooted it to Hollywood and made *I Know What You Did Last Summer*. But of course the current name on everyone's lips is award-winning short filmmaker Andrea Arnold whose debut feature *Red Road* won the Jury prize in Cannes, amongst many others.

But it does seem that short film allows filmmakers to be more independent and take more chances, and once they move to features, that independence is taken away.

What advice do you have for novice filmmakers planning to make a short?

I suppose the best advice is to stay true to yourself – make it for you and no one else. We get fed up with short films acting as calling cards to get into the industry, proving what they can do rather than concentrating on a truthful and honest piece of work.

INTERVIEW WITH JOE BATEMAN (FESTIVAL DIRECTOR)

Rushes, which began in 1977, is one of the world's leading visual effects houses. Rushes Soho Shorts Festival is an annual event for the work of both established filmmakers and newcomers. www.sohoshorts.com

How did Rushes Soho Shorts Festival come about?

The festival was born from a 'pub' night out. Over a few pints of beer a group of frustrated filmmaking colleagues bemoaned the lack of a Soho-based festival celebrating material that was being created in the area. During the course of the evening they put a simple plan together and over the following weeks contacted everyone who they thought would be interested. They found nothing but support. All employed at Rushes, they decided to work around their day jobs to put the idea into action.

How do you see the festival in the context of other short film festivals?

Being in the centre of London we are very much the focus of the local production community. As such we've earned a reputation for being a festival to be seen in if you want to be commissioned to make commercials, promos and advertisements. Our programme is certainly more mainstream and less experimental than most festivals. Our core programme is the six competition categories, which highlights work made in the previous year. We are also very aware of the number of other film festivals out there and look to provide a platform for those festivals by screening their latest winning films and showcase programmes. As with most film festivals we want to provide a showcase programme, highlighting and profiling work we believe should be seen, alongside networking and educational events that generate further projects and productions.

Does the festival specialise in certain genres of shorts?

Yes. We look at titles sequences, animation, documentary and music promos as well as the fictional short films. We have a broad range of experience showcased in the festival and so we also have our newcomer category, which allows us to highlight the best of the entry-level filmmakers.

How long does the festival run for?

So far we've run over a period of one week from the last Saturday in July to the first Friday in August, but this is likely to change in the future as we've already begun to run out of space.

Have you seen an increase in the amount of people submitting and attending the festival over the last few years?

Definitely. Each year we have a steadily rising number of submissions and people attending the festival. With the expansion of our programme, 2007 sees the addition of the Documentary category, and with the development of a number of other initiatives and strategies over the next few years we hope to further increase our audience on a global level.

What kind of people do you have on your judging panel?

We have a large and varied judging panel. Each judge is very experienced in their particular field whether they are a film critic, magazine editor, commissioning editor, artistic director, director, actor, comedian, sales agent, production manager, casting director, programmer or producer.

SUBMITTING TO FESTIVALS

Most festivals, whether large or small, will have a website. Beyond gauging whether the film festival looks suitable and the deadline for submissions, you will also be able to download their application form and carefully check the requirements of entry. This can be filled in and sent along with a preview copy of your film on DVD, which will be screened by the selection panel. If accepted, a screening copy will be requested. Various festivals require different formats for screening. Conventionally the most common formats are 35mm, DigiBeta and DVD. When sending either a preview copy of your film or the screening copy, always ensure it's clearly labelled. If you are entering an international festival, check which video format they require the preview and screening copies to be in. Different countries may require PAL, NTSC or SECAM. In addition to the information you give on the submission form, you should also supply some kind of info sheet or press kit. This can take any form you like and can be as lavish or mundane as you want, but it should contain as much useful information about your film as possible. The following is a useful list of info that you should try and supply:

- Title, running time, screening formats
- Synopsis, theme
- Director/producer contact details
- Cast and crew list
- Production stills/film stills
- List of other festivals where it has screened
- Any press or reviews of the film

ONLINE SUBMISSION

Conventionally film festival submission has consisted of finding suitable festivals, keeping track of deadlines, filling out submission forms as well as physically posting them all off; a process both time-consuming and difficult to organise. But now this standard method is undergoing a significant change. The last few years have seen the arrival of new Internet-based resources that not only give you comprehensive lists and information on film festivals, but also allow you to apply online.

At the most basic level these companies allow you to avoid endless form filling, but still require you to send the DVD preview. However, several companies now allow you to upload a preview-quality digital file of your film, so that it can then be viewed by the relevant selection panels to make their decision. This entirely removes the need to send anything except the screening copy if your film is selected. Although this is a new occurrence, with many film festivals still following the traditional method, this is the future of film festival submission.

Beyond hugely simplifying the submission process and reducing the hours you would spend queuing at the post office, companies also allow you to create a custom profile for your film, so that you can automatically filter and categorise the types of festival you want to submit to, and upload an online press kit, with extra information and stills of your film.

At present three of the most established online submission sites are:

www.withoutabox.com
www.reelport.com
www.shortfilmdepot.com

INTERVIEW WITH JOE NEULIGHT (FESTIVAL DISTRIBUTION)

Joe Neulight and David Strauss set up Withoutabox.com in order to facilitate the film festival submission process. With over 1,000 film festivals taking place every year, finding submission deadlines and organising an application strategy has conventionally been a nightmarish task. Withoutabox.com has developed a revolutionary service that allows you to search out the festivals that you want to apply to via their extensive database and create a profile for your film. Amongst the many features offered, you can create your own online schedule with automated email reminders and upload online press kits that can be accessed by festival organisers. It's an indispensable resource for most short filmmakers.

What inspired you to set up Withoutabox?

Withoutabox was born of adversity and necessity while my partner, David Strauss, and I were filmmakers ourselves, attempting to untangle the world of festivals on paper, in an analogue world. We knew there had to be a better way, and the Internet afforded it. We also felt that by bringing the world of independent filmmakers together in one place, we could help spearhead a movement to democratise film distribution and give more self-determination and expression to filmmakers through emerging and traditional distribution channels. Now the site has 100,000 filmmakers in 200 countries, listings of thousands of festivals around the world, with more opportunities and features rolling out every month.

Figure 56. Withoutabox website. www.withoutabox.com

So if a director had just completed a short film how would they go about using Withoutabox?

It's pretty easy, and 3,000 new films a month do it. Just create a free account on the site and input all the data common to festival entry forms into one master project form. After that there are clever ways to search out the right festivals for your film, helpful weekly deadline updates and automated reminders you can set. When you find a festival you want, you just click and apply. If there's an entry fee, you can pay it online. Users can also upload press kit contents and other marketing materials free and put a trailer online free, through our relationship with Google. And starting in October you'll also be able to send us a copy of your DVD and we'll take care of getting your screeners out – for a reasonable fee through our relationship with US-based CustomFlix – so it can be a 'fully clickable service', with nothing to touch once you are set up.

Filmmakers have an option to pay for an annual subscription package, which gets them discounts on every festival to which they submit, plus a bunch of other bonuses. We're happy for filmmakers to use it free, though.

Filmmakers are also encouraged to create a public marketing page on our social networking platform, called Audience by Withoutabox, to start the process of amassing a following before, during and after the festival circuit. This becomes a great asset in distribution or self-distribution, for which we are forging new ways and efficiencies as well. Audience – found at http://audience.withoutabox.com/ – is growing fast. Festivals are beginning to use Audience to post their complete schedules, manage ticket sales, and encourage audience participation and feedback as part of the festival process. It integrates seamlessly with the submission system for filmmakers and festivals, so when you are set up in one, you are ready to go with the other.

Does the director need to have previously shown at film festivals to use Withoutabox?

Absolutely not. We have everyone from Academy Award™ winners to first-timers using the site, even kid filmmakers submitting to youth sections of film festivals. It's for anyone with any kind of film. Festivals are looking to discover; that's their job, and that's what we facilitate at all levels. The people who use Withoutabox are naturally the ones who want to take their work seriously and take it the next step to market, which is to say it's not – by nature – hobby or 'throw-away' content (à la 'user generated content').

What else would you need to supply apart from a finished version of the film?

The finished version of the film is actually not required, unless you want Withoutabox to send out your screeners for you. Filmmakers themselves decide how much they want to do and how much they want Withoutabox to do, and base their set up on that. At minimum, they need to fill out the entry form. Everything else is optional. The more filmmakers do via Withoutabox, the easier it is on the festivals, because it lets them focus on watching films instead of administering submissions.

Do you specialise in certain kinds of film festivals or genres of film?

We run the gambit. Film festivals have proliferated more than 300% in the last five years, and Withoutabox has helped make that possible. We're the first ones to say that not every film is for every festival, but it would be hard to imagine a film that could not find a home among our enormous list of partners.

Do you have a quality control system for films that use Withoutabox?

Withoutabox is not a filter; it's just a tool. Festivals want it that way, and so do filmmakers. We're a matchmaking system, but we don't control the match, the users control it.

Do you have any advice for first-time short filmmakers who have never shown at festivals before and are trying to work out which ones to submit to?

We encourage filmmakers to study the offering a bit and submit to the festivals that seem to fit the profile of their film. There are different reasons for applying to different festivals. Some are to attract industry and reach into the market. Some are more to get your work in front of regional audiences and play to 'real people'. Some are in your mum's hometown so she can bring her friends to see what you've done. Some give you an excuse to travel to far off lands (which we always found to be the best way to travel – with a film). Others offer ancillary distribution or large cash prizes to winners. Our Short List feature can help to intelligently narrow the field as soon as a filmmaker puts in their film info. And narrowing is half the battle.

DISTRIBUTION COMPANIES

Beyond self-distributing your own film via festivals and associated markets, there are a growing number of short film distribution companies that market and distribute a select range of short films. With access to clients in search of short films whether for television broadcast, Internet entertainment or pod casting, these companies act as sales agents for short filmmakers, taking on commercially viable films and potentially making a profit for both the company and the filmmaker. Distribution companies will normally take a percentage of any revenue from the sale of a film, ranging from 20% to 40%. Distributors will generally require exclusive rights to distribute the film for a prescribed number of years, either for worldwide distribution or specific territories.

Distribution companies can be submitted to directly, but often select the majority of their films from screenings at major international short film festivals.

MARKETS

Theatrical release

Traditionally the commercial potential for most short films has been fairly limited due to their length. Outside of film festivals there has never really been a demand for theatrical screenings of short films and this market has conventionally been small to non-existent.

Television

Starting in the mid-1980s with the advent of cable and satellite channels, television broadcast has been by far the largest commercial market for short films, with most sales being made to television channels have consistent programming slots for shorts. Television channels source most of their acquisitions from the international film festival markets and from distribution companies, and these sales have largely been responsible for the possibility of directors and producers reaping financial rewards from their work.

Internet

The Internet, in particular broadband streaming, is having a massive impact on short film distribution. Whether it's filmmakers who are setting up their own websites for their films, or companies like AtomFilms providing entire libraries of short films as downloadable entertainment, the Internet is potentially offering short filmmakers the biggest audiences ever.

With AtomFilms leading the way in successfully showcasing short films online, generating profit from advertising rather than sale of the actual shorts, it looks as if the Internet market might become the largest short film market ever.

Figure 57.
AtomFilms website.
www.atomfilms.com

New technologies

Both mobile phones and iPods potentially offer short films a new arena for distribution. Podcasts and downloads are perfectly suited to short form films, and it's no coincidence that both Nokia and Orange have set up their own short film competitions; Nokia's for 15-second films and Orange's for 60-second films. iTunes are also beginning to offer short films for download. Similar to the rapidly expanding online market, these new technologies look set to become a potentially huge market for shorts.

DVD

Although a single short film release on DVD is rarely a commercially viable option, compilations are becoming increasingly popular. The series of *Cinema 16* compilations (European, British and American) have compiled series of shorts by renowned feature and short film directors. Major festivals are also beginning to release their own annual compilations, with onedotzero now on their fifth release and Raindance festival also bringing out compilations of shorts.

INTERVIEW WITH DAVID RUSSELL (SHORT FILM DISTRIBUTION)

David Russell set up Big Film Shorts in 1996 as an exclusively short film distribution company. Big Film Shorts acts both as a sales agent for the films in their catalogue and also as consultants for film bookers and programmers.

What inspired you to set up Big Film Shorts?

Ten years ago I attended the Palm Springs Short Film Festival and saw lots of people paying $5 to see films with no stars and I thought something might be going to happen for the short form in the industry.

What kind of markets and territories do you distribute to?

We contract to represent films in all markets:

Theatrical (very little opportunity here)
Television (we license to channels around the world on all continents)
DVD (we do some collections for manufacturer/distributors, mostly in the US)
Internet/broadband (any licence to do with this is worldwide)
Non-theatrical (schools, libraries, airlines, military, hotels etc)

Figure 58. Big Film Shorts website.

Do you find that there is more market interest in shorts now than say ten years ago?

Absolutely. I knew it would come eventually. It's just taken longer than I hoped. But the general market, particularly the new technologies, are finally focusing on shorts, and we are launching our own video on demand channel, called NANO, on Comcast cable in October.

Do you see new markets emerging with the advent of new technologies like podcasting?

Yes, they are emerging. It's hard to tell yet if they are going to be the big break short films need. We're hopeful. Certainly there is interest from many to get short films for free but this all could develop into real paying markets in the future.

Where do you find the films that you pick up for distribution?

Festivals and markets such as Palm Springs, Aspen, Toronto Shortsfest, and Clermont-Ferrand. Referrals from other filmmakers. Over-the-transom blind submissions.

How do you go about selecting the films that you choose to distribute?

We look for films that we hope will be commercially viable, in all genres, for our worldwide clients. And they have to be legally cleared for commercial exhibition, as opposed to just festival play.

Do you specialise in certain genres of short?

We don't, but the market does, hence we have to focus more on comedies and strong dramas.

Do you find certain types of film easier to distribute than others?

Of course, the genres of sci-fi, horror, action and celebrity fall under the broad categories of comedy and/or drama.

How long can you distribute a film for before it's exhausted?

If the film stands up and is not dated then the shelf life can be ongoing for years and years.

What does a director or producer stand to gain from having their film picked up for distribution?

Hopefully, a distributor can take care of the selling of the film, which takes years and lots of time, leaving the director to go on with making more films.

Is it possible to make a financially viable short, where the director and producer not only cover the costs of making it but also make a profit?

It's possible and does happen occasionally, but it's a buyer's market and they don't pay well for short form content. There are at least 5,000+ new short films made every year.

Do you have any advice for filmmakers looking to get their film distributed?

Make it short (3-12 minutes) and make sure they have all clearances in writing so they can legally sell their film. Not very glamorous or sexy, but essential to getting a film sold.

31. THE DIRECTORS

INTERVIEW WITH AMANDA BOYLE (DIRECTOR)

Amanda Boyle wrote and directed *Hotel Infinity*, which features on the accompanying DVD. Now focusing on her directing career, she is also a highly sought after producer, due to her experience in developing and producing both short and feature-length films.

How did you get involved in short filmmaking?

Like many kids I was really into amateur dramatics – it started with acting and then progressed into directing. At university I did a lot of plays and after three years realised that what I really wanted to do was direct film. I can't remember what prompted that revelation, possibly a month of acting with a glove puppet at the Edinburgh Fringe.

I started writing letters to film production companies to try to get a job and also began working on student short films. After several hundred letters, I eventually got a job at Working Title Films. I stayed with them for about three years and then spent a further four years developing a slate of projects with the producer Jon Finn, still under the umbrella of Working Title, for a small stable of directors that included Stephen Daldry.

How did your experience with film production transfer into directing a short?

I was lucky I met Jon Finn at Working Title because with him I worked in both production and development. I got a complete overview of the filmmaking process. He is a very creative producer so we were always talking about films as a whole – what we were trying to make and how we might achieve that. I also got to observe a variety of talented directors.

At the same time I was writing short films and doing evening/weekend cours-es. It wasn't that my experience with film production transferred into directing a short... I always wanted to direct, I just had some weird notion that I had to understand every area of film before I could do so. In retrospect that was prob-ably a delaying tactic as I was timid of starting.

What gave you the idea for *Hotel Infinity*?

A children's book on infinity, which I found in the Science Museum bookshop.

How long did it take you to develop the script?

Something silly like a year. I was still using delaying tactics...

At what stage did you start working with producer Adrian Sturges?

Once I had a script I was happy with, I started to put together a crew. I spoke to various people about producing the film. Robin Gutch at FilmFour suggested Adrian. It was a relief to find him. I wouldn't have been able to make the film without him. He is hard working and great fun.

What was the budget for the film and how did you go about raising the finances for it?

The budget was 60k – 50k of which Adrian raised from private financiers and 10k from the UK Film Council's Completion Fund.

How long did you spend on pre-production for the film?

Ages – another year maybe? It took a while to raise the money.

How did you go about casting for the film? Did you use a casting agent?

Adrian introduced me to Tara Woodward and Tamara Gillon. They found me a dream cast.

How did you find your DP? What made you choose Hubert Taczanowski?

I met him on *My Little Eye*, which I had worked on at Working Title. He agreed to it when we were out filming in the freezing cold of Nova Scotia and I cruelly held him to his word. He has an amazing eye and is incredibly experienced; he has shot over 15 features. Working with him on this short was basically like going to film school. The way the film looks is very much down to him as well

Figure 59. Film still from Amanda Boyle's *Hotel Infinity*.

as Jacqueline Abrahams (the production designer), Mags Arnold (editor), Sam
Perry (costume) and Ben Smith (CGI at The Mill).

**Did you look into shooting the film on other formats? What made you choose
35mm?**

I did think about Super 16mm but chose 35mm in the end because we got the
budget. I also hoped it might entice Hubert.

How did you find your crew for the film?

Most of the crew were people I had met at Working Title or who Adrian had
worked with before or who were highly recommended by friends.

How long did it take to shoot?

One day in Switzerland and three days in Bethnal Green.

Did you encounter any major problems on the shoot?

It snowed overnight in Switzerland – so all the places we had recced looked
completely different. That turned out to be a happy accident as the fog and
snow defined the look of the film. I now can't imagine it not looking like that.

How did the experience of working on a short film differ to the feature films you have worked on?

I had always been passionate about the features I had worked on but it's a different experience directing. It's a terrific high.

Being your first experience of directing, how did you develop your approach to directing actors?

I wouldn't say I had an approach. I winged it. The actors were very patient with me but it frustrated me as I felt I needed a technique and that I should have prepared better. That's the area I have worked hardest on since to develop.

How did the fact that you were going to use digital visual effects in your post influence the way that you shot the film?

It didn't really as most of those shots are separate from the action. We just had to shoot the corridor/dining room scenes in chunks and then they were stitched together digitally.

What kind of workflow did you follow for the post-production stages?

A wait-until-people-have-time kind of workflow. We relied on favours in post.

How long did the post-production take?

Mags Arnold cut the film over the Christmas holiday (we shot the film in September) and then we waited until The Mill had space to do the CGI. I think we finished the following March.

When you came to edit did you realise that there were other shots you would have liked to have got?

Absolutely. We had no coverage, we just didn't have time. In many scenes we only had one way to cut the scene.

At what stage did you start working with the composer, Christopher Benstead? How closely did you work with him on the score?

I worked with a music supervisor, Gabriel Crouch, who had devised the music for a one-woman show I did at university and is now a classical musician. After much hunting, Gabriel found a Finnish folk tune, which seemed to capture the essence of the film and appears in its entirety at the end. He asked Chris Benstead, a specialist in composing music for contemporary dance, to weave that melody into a soundtrack. Chris created a totally unique score that completely enhanced the film.

What did you do with the film once it was completed? Did you have a strategy for distributing the film before you started making it?

Adrian introduced me to Dawn at Dazzle who has done a brilliant job at distributing the film.

What has come out of showing it at film festivals etc?

We have won a couple of awards and the film has been seen around the world from Russia to Utah to Abu Dhabi.

What did you learn from your experiences making *Hotel Infinity*? In retrospect, are there any things that you would have done differently?

Now I probably would have made it darker and funnier. I would have made the script less mysterious. The film was always a clear metaphor for me about grief and I think I was rather cautious of making that explicit.

What did you do after completing *Hotel Infinity*?

I gradually began to focus on directing. I am now prepping *Imprint* written by Kate Hardie, a 30-minute drama for Channel 4 under their Coming Up scheme; and developing a new short film based on the celebrated short story *Pop Art* by Joe Hill, as well as writing my first feature, *Generation*.

What advice do you have for filmmakers considering making a short?

Find a story you like, collect together a great team of people and make it!

What do you enjoy most about making short films?

I love the form of short films. You have so much freedom. They are a fantastic chance to experiment.

INTERVIEW WITH LAURENCE CORIAT (DIRECTOR)

Laurence Coriat is a renowned screenwriter who has written numerous feature films including *Me Without You* directed by Sandra Goldbacher and *Wonderland* directed by Michael Winterbottom. She has also written and directed several shorts, and her directorial debut, *Being Bad*, is featured on the accompanying DVD.

Figure 60. Film still from Laurence Coriat's *Being Bad.*

How did you get involved in short filmmaking?

I started off as a scriptwriter but was always deep down really interested in directing. Finally I built up enough confidence and decided to try it out to see if I liked it and if I was any good at it. Making a short film was the best way to find out.

How has your experience as a screenwriter for feature film influenced your approach to making shorts?

It's made me feel more confident to break the rules and take risks. As a writer you know the material so well that it allows you to be more flexible to change things once you are actually making the film.

Where did the inspiration come from for *Being Bad*?

When I decided that writing scripts wasn't enough for me, I thought I should either direct films or write a novel (because a novel is a finished product). So I started with the novel (it doesn't cost any money) and I started writing the story of three teenage kids (two boys and a girl) who were orphans in an orphanage and how they formed a 'ménage a trois' and re-created the family which they never had. I enjoyed writing but directing was still niggling at me and so I decided to turn the ten first pages of the novel into the short that then became *Being Bad*.

How long did it take to develop the script?

It didn't take any time at all. I had already written it as a piece of prose in a 'poetic' kind of way so I just kept the same tone for the script. I didn't want to make a typical short film so I thought that should be reflected in the writing also.

How did you go about raising finance for it?

Since this wasn't going to be a typical short film it was difficult for me to find a 'classical' producer. I tried but most people I know are involved in feature films and aren't really interested in short films. I got a bit frustrated and didn't really want to wait around too long to get the money through the normal channels and so in the end I decided to put up my own money and just go and do it off the cuff. Then I needed someone who spoke French and someone recommended Amy who had just come back from Japan. She was very enthusiastic and really up for it. She came in more like a line producer/production manager in the end. Then when the film was finished and got into Sundance I needed some money to make a 35mm print and I found more people who put money up for the blow up.

How did you go about casting for the film?

Most of the actual pre-production time was spent casting. We did both some 'wild' casting and also talked to a Marseille casting agent. So we found Malik in the street (he had no experience in film at all), and then the other boy and the girl were recommended to me by the casting director in Marseille. We filmed them together and the chemistry worked...

I got my cinematographer (Natasha Braier) and editor (Ida Bregninge) here in London out of the film school and we hit it off straightaway. We made the film with no lights and minimal crew and with barely any pre-production.

How did you come to choose Natasha Braier as a DOP?

Natasha was recommended to me through someone I was working with as a scriptwriter, who thought we would get on. I saw her reel and loved it and met her and we connected immediately. And when we made the film, it went beyond my expectations. I really felt it was a perfect collaboration. She has the kind of sensibility and eye that completely match with mine. And that's very exciting.

Did you have a very distinct look in mind or did that evolve in the shoot?

Both. I had a lot of references which I discussed with Natasha (mostly Claire Denis' *Beau Travail*) and the work of Chris Doyle. But then things totally evolved with the shoot. I learned that wide shots aren't really great with DV and so you have to adapt. And I also love the way Natasha works with what she has got around her because that's what I am like too. So not everything is planned but you see something that strikes you or a certain natural light and you just go for it. And sometimes that's the best shot we got. The unplanned ones. But of course you have a strong frame of reference to start off with.

Did you look into shooting the film on other formats?

We shot the film on a Sony PD 150, so on DV format. Because the script read as such a 'textured' film it would have made sense to try and shoot on film but my aim was to go and shoot it quickly, and off the cuff, and DV lets you do that.

How did you find your crew for the film?

Recommendations. I had someone who was going to be my first AD in Marseille, who dropped me at the last minute as he got offered a feature film (paid). I must have been lucky that I just found people at the last minute from a list that was given to me of all the technicians in Marseille. Maybe it helped that it is a smaller place than London and also in France they have a different system which allows people to work on short films: they have to do so many hours and then the government pays for them, taking into account that they may not be working all the time. But it was a very tiny crew. And then once people are onboard they always know someone who knows someone. Natasha also had some connections of her own, which helped out at the last minute.

How long did it take to shoot?

We shot it over four or five days. But not full days. Maybe three full days and then some bits and pieces in the night. Because they were kids we didn't really film late. And also according to the weather we moved scenes around.

Did you follow a storyboard closely or did you improvise?

No, no storyboard (I can't draw!). I have a strong sense of what the feel of a scene needs to be but then from that point I feel completely open to let things develop. And I love accidents and the totally unexpected things that inevitably happen, so the process is both controlled and free at once.

As your first experience of directing actors, how did you develop your approach?

Because they are teenagers, even if they have a little film or TV experience they are still fresh and it's still possible to capture something pretty raw and 'real' from them. I think it's a question of trust and building an atmosphere of trust so that they feel comfortable trying things out. But we also got a lot of 'stolen moments' when they were not aware they were being filmed. If you let the camera roll (which you can do in DV) they finally let go and do things that they may not do after saying 'action', which I try to avoid saying because I think it just freezes everyone.

Also in the way you cast, you get a certain quality in them that you know will show on screen so they don't have to 'act' so much.

How long did the post-production take?

I can't really remember but we probably edited for about two weeks all in all and then we did some online and grading (as little as we could as it's so expensive!). For *Being Bad* there was no real sound dub till we made the 35mm print.

How creative was the editing process? Did you just cut it as you had planned or did the film take on a different shape in editing?

Well again it's like for the filming, it's both. The editing was very creative and kept at the core emotion and ideas of the original script but we moved things around. Ida is as much a collaborator as Natasha. I think the film is a result of our three-way team. That's because our sensibilities match completely.

How did you find the composer Ben Foster and how closely did you work with him on the score?

We put an ad out in film schools and music schools mentioning Georges Dele-rue (a French composer who composed the best film music ever for Godard's *Le Mépris*) and Ben responded that he loved his work. So we met and Ben came up with some ideas. Ben is a great musician and composer, and for me what is more difficult is trying to explain in terms of music what I was looking for. It's hard. You say 'a bit more sad', 'a bit less romantic' but it's hard to make yourself understood. In the end we kept the beginning part of the wonderful theme Ben came up with and put it in a loop because after the end bit it became too big and too romantic for the film. But it's very hard to say to a composer 'I only want the first bit'. It must be frustrating for them. Also it's hard to know before you put the image and the music together how exactly it's going to work. You can have an idea but sometimes you may be surprised.

Did you find that the finished film was very close to how you had imagined it when you were writing the script?

Yes and no. Yes because it created a certain 'world', which I very much had in mind. And no because I don't really ever imagine the film so very precisely when I write it. I imagine a 'texture' and a 'mood' rather than a set of precise elements.

How did your experience working on a short film differ to the feature films you have worked on?

Well the feature films I worked on I worked as a scriptwriter not as a director. But in my mind I decided to approach the short just the same way as I would approach the feature. And in a way I think I could very much write *Being Bad* as a feature film too. I think the characters have enough depth to be developed for a feature film. But since it was a short, I felt it would be a snapshot of those characters and those lives.

What did you do with the film once it was completed? Did you have a strategy for distributing it before you started making it?

I didn't have any strategy at all beforehand. I knew very little about short films. I made the film to see whether I would enjoy directing and whether I would be good at it, so when the film was finished and people liked it, it went beyond all my expectations. And it was great to see that a short film could have a life. It got accepted by the British Council who sent it to festivals and it started doing pretty well and then Dawn Sharpless at Dazzle films, who distributes short films, took it on and sold it to Channel 4 and Sundance Channel. But I guess because

I don't really have a producer, it's a lot of work – to send it to festivals, fill in forms all by myself – so sometimes I perhaps don't do all the things I should be doing for it. But I do feel it's had a good life.

What has come out of showing the film at festivals etc?

It's very encouraging that people really like the film a lot. It made me want to do another one. And perhaps it has been the start of people starting to think of me as a director (but I had to make another perhaps more 'classically' narrative short to capitalise on this even more). But I think you have to win prizes for it to make such a difference…

What did you learn from your experiences making *Being Bad*? In retrospect are there any things you would have done differently?

Of course there are always things you would do differently but I don't find that a useful way to think about things. On the other hand, I learned a hell of a lot by making it. But every time you make a film you learn something new, and every film is different so you learn something different.

Maybe the most useful thing I learned is that there isn't one way of doing things. Or one way of directing. I used to think I couldn't direct because I didn't always know so clearly what I wanted but I realised I do know what I want but I don't express it by making storyboards or precise shot lists etc.

What did you do after completing *Being Bad*?

I wanted to make another short straightaway to see whether it was a fluke that I enjoyed directing so much and that the film had turned out okay… and I did make another short called *Holiday* and it was as exciting and turned out okay too.

What are your plans for the future?

I continue working as a scriptwriter for other directors but I have a feature film I hope to direct and I am writing more projects for myself too.

What advice do you have for filmmakers considering making a short?

Be bold, take risks. Make the film you really want to make and know where your strengths are. Remember that some things may be perceived as flaws but they may become your strengths… because it's what will make you stand out.

What do you enjoy the most about making short films?

Well for me it's been the freedom, because I have been able to finance them myself.

INTERVIEW WITH CHARLES HENDLEY (DIRECTOR)

Charles Hendley has directed two short films *Dead Flies Are No Good* and *Shelf Life*. He has numerous film projects in development, in both long and short formats, and also directs commercials. *Shelf Life* is featured on the accompanying DVD.

How did you get involved in short filmmaking?

Simply as a means of demonstrating my abilities as a director – to direct narrative. Doing commercials is fine, but it's quite rare to find a script that allows you to do everything you want to do. Short films give you that opportunity.

Did you have much previous experience?

I didn't go to film school. I actually studied economics at university. I personally found that the moment I started making films, I just grasped it. I seemed to understand it. It's about having a three-dimensional mind.

Was *Shelf Life* your first film?

Apart from commercials, this was the first film I had done.

What gave you the idea?

I saw a cartoon in Germany, which was 2D. It was a guy with blood coming out of his head saying, 'Be careful in the home'. It was by Nils Alzen; I gave him a credit on the film. I thought it was a cute concept. What I love doing is withholding information, until a certain moment, so that people don't quite understand what's going on, or think they do but then discover it's actually something else.

It's a form of irony, I suppose, which is very apparent in the work of Hitchcock. I'm always on the look out for scenarios like that.

How long did it take to write the script?

The first version was knocked out in a couple of days, and then over time as the process developed different ideas accumulated. Subsequently, the art director had the idea of making him a safety expert. We were originally just going to have him hanging a picture on the wall but she came up with the idea of it being a safety certificate, which added some irony. I also added little clues about death, like the six raw plugs being six bullets and the cross he makes on the wall being like cross hairs.

Did you storyboard quite heavily?

Yes we did, although you can't control every single thing that happens and you shouldn't. The thing with short films is that there's never enough time. You have to make absolutely the most of every single moment you have. I like playing around with funny angles, so that when you put the camera there, some people aren't sure if you've crossed the line. I still don't actually know what that means. I remember with the feet stepping on to the mat, half of you thinks, 'That can't be right', but with the movement of the guy's body, it just works.

How much did it cost to make?

It didn't cost much, less than £1,000. It's always down to the wonderful generosity of the people involved. But there is a certain amount of self-interest too as everyone can put it on their own reels. If you can make it good then everyone is going to be proud of it and get some credit.

How long did you spend on pre-production?

It all happened very quickly. The biggest problem was finding where to do it. A friend had a neighbour who was having their house rebuilt, and there was one room that was just plaster and looked right.

How did you end up casting Michael Winner?

We just thought, 'Who might deserve getting it most?' So we faxed his management company and they faxed back and said he was up for it. We told them we would do it whenever he wanted. He was very charming and he actually came up with the formula for the blood: tomato ketchup.

How long did the shoot take?

Just a day, quite a short one. I managed to get everything I needed.

How about the post-production?

About three or four weeks. It all happened very quickly too. It was very close to what I had imagined, which is about as good as you can get.

What was your approach to directing?

Well you can't have a trademark, you have to look at the material and try and reflect that. The wonderful thing about being a director is that you have all these different dimensions that you can play with to communicate the message, and the message is the emotion. It's the emotions that count. With short films it's hard to do that because you don't know the characters for long enough and they don't do things that really matter.

It's very hard to be emotionally involved in two or three minutes, but nevertheless the material still dictates what you do and the choices you make. If you don't feel it then it's very hard to do it intellectually. It really comes down to casting, everything is casting. And you're not just casting the actors, you are casting the crew too. Once you get that right, you don't need to tell people what to do.

What did you learn from the experience of making it?

I reconfirmed my suspicion that I really like making movies, and I'm still trying to make them; I'm still writing.

Do you have any advice for new filmmakers?

Keep doing it as much as possible. The longer you do it for, the luckier you get. Always take the opportunity to shoot, and be good at it.

INTERVIEW WITH TOBY ROBERTS (DIRECTOR)

After studying film and television at the University of California, Toby Roberts began a successful screenwriting career, before returning to the UK to focus on directing his own projects. His output has ranged from a feature-length mockumentary to a truly short film. Clocking in at just over 15 seconds, *Chrysanthemums the Word* is featured on the accompanying DVD.

Figure 61. Film still from Toby Roberts' *Chrysanthemums the Word*.

How did you get involved in short filmmaking?

My father works in the film industry so we always had a video camera of one sort or another around the house, even in the days of the old half-inch VHS cameras. My fascination with filming therefore began by watching and making home videos. Over time, I developed a sense of the values of lighting, framing and movement, in the process of fooling around with mates making rock-videos, silly sketches, filming parties and the like.

I suppose my first 'proper' short film was *Wivenhoe: Taking Up the Arts*. I'd bumped into an old friend of mine, pop-poet Martin Newell, who was working on a mockumentary about Wivenhoe, the bohemian Essex riverside town I was brought up in. He asked if I'd like to get involved and I ended up directing it. We had some silly ideas, very little money and a community of people who were up for taking the piss out of themselves on camera. It was great. And a complete luxury because we had no time restraints, no pressure from executives, no big film crews creating obstacles. Just us, a few friends and quite a lot of drinks. I've been trying to emulate that in my films ever since.

The film ran in at around 30 minutes. We set up a fabulous publicity stunt by creating Wivenhoe's first film premiere. We got in touch with absolutely everybody we knew and told them to come along and then called the national newspapers and local media hyping it up to be a massive local celeb fest. Sadly, and not altogether surprisingly, none of the big papers turned up, but most of the local ones did. A good 200–300 people gathered outside the venue. We glammed it up by bringing in the cast and crew in limousines, although we only had two. We all met at a house close to the venue and then each limo took one or two people, dropped them off outside the venue and then came back to pick up the others, each one going round several times altogether. We had friends dress up as chauffeurs and bouncers keeping the public away from the 'stars' as they disembarked. The bouncers had homemade ear-pieces that they pretended to talk to some security HQ through. And the red carpet came from someone's bathroom... it even had a cut out at one end where the loo went! Three local mayors greeted the stars from the limos and ushered them towards the film crew. We'd borrowed a Sony DSR-250 and a redhead light and held brief 'interviews' before they waved to the crowd and went inside. We didn't actually have any tape in the camera. Most of the press took it all, as they should have, very light-heartedly – writing about people like Harrison Ford being upset that he hadn't got an invite etc. But one or two of them thought the whole thing was serious, saying that there had been nothing like this in Wivenhoe ever before. It was a resounding success and we very nearly made our money back! I think they're still selling the DVDs in the Wivenhoe bookshop today.

Where did the inspiration come from for *Chrysanthemums the Word*?

My father wrote the poem many years ago. He was bos'n on a boat heading for the Mediterranean and was on watch with the steward who was entertaining Dad with a story about an argument he'd had with his girlfriend. Neither of them admitted fault or defeat. Then, several days later, she thanked him for the flowers he'd sent, they ended up in bed together and the whole thing was seemingly forgotten. However, while he was happy about the outcome of the disagreement, the steward was still puzzled, as well as concerned, about the flowers... you see, he'd never actually sent her any. So, on the long night watch the steward and the bos'n wrote the poem.

My dad sent me the poem a year or two back in an email. I kept it and would occasionally read it for a laugh. Then, in the summer of 2005, I came across the 15-second film festival online, sponsored by Nokia. Like many, I was intrigued how you could possibly make a film so short. Then I remembered the poem, re-read it with a stopwatch, and decided I would turn it into a film.

Did you always envision it as one shot, or did you consider other ways of making it?

It's always been a one-shot film in my mind although the focus of the shot went through a number of changes. Originally I had it in mind to start at the foot of the bed with her legs, face down, poking out from under the duvet. Then we'd track up the bed to the only head on the pillow: his, enjoying the pleasure she was providing... until he suddenly realises that he hadn't sent any flowers. He does this now with a more subtle glance to camera.

Roughly how long did you spend on pre-production for the film?

As I recall, I spent remarkably little time in pre-production. This is one of the beautiful things of working on such a short film with one location, a crew of three and no budget. Once I'd got the location and the equipment, I'd say most of the time was spent discussing the camera movement. We were maybe two or three weeks in pre-production, but if you added all the time actually spent working on the film, it would probably fit into a single working day.

How did you come to choose Simon Reed as DP?

Actually, he came to me. He's a local filmmaker and a friend who'd recently purchased a Sony Z1. He'd very kindly offered his services with the camera. I think he was keen to try it out on a project other than his own so that he could focus solely on the camerawork for a change. He's normally a director.

What was the budget and how did you raise the finances?

We had no money. Actually, I spent £3 on a DV tape, but that was it. This is the beauty of modern filmmaking; once you've got the equipment you can start making films. And the equipment is so much cheaper than 10 or 20 years ago. I don't recall exactly how we raised the £3, but I imagine it was self-financed.

Which format did you shoot on and did you look into shooting the film on other formats?

We filmed it on MiniDV. We'd considered shooting on HDV as we had the Z1 but Simon the DP decided against it – quite why, I don't recall – and I was happy to go along with it. I think I was more eager to get the film made than spend time worrying about the format.

How long did it take to shoot?

We spent a couple of hours setting up the jib and rehearsing the shot and probably another couple of hours filming it.

Did you have that particular camera move in mind prior to the shoot?

The camera move I had in mind is the camera move you see: a rotating crane shot. The more prepared you are with a shooting script the better the day will go and therefore the better the film will look. To go into a shoot without any ideas on your camera movements is suicide.

How many takes did you do, to get 'The One'?

I honestly can't remember. Maybe about 20 to 30 if you include the incomplete shots. It was a lot because we had difficulty with the jib. The Z1 didn't fit onto it correctly, so we had to rig it up so that the camera was on the outside of the housing. As Gary Leach, the grip, lowered the camera end of the jib, Simon had to account for the perpetually changing angle of camera with a remote. To make things worse, the remote was attached to the head of the jib with a short cable, so as well as trying to get the shot right, he was clambering over the actors in the bed to prevent the cable from pulling taut. The shot that made it into the film was the only one that was perfect.

So how did you find directing and acting in your own film?

I loved it. But it was only a one-shot film. It would be far more complex on a bigger movie. That said, I would relish the challenge. Besides, I think the only acting jobs I'll get are in my own films.

How long did the post-production take?

Having filmed in the afternoon, we edited in the evening at Simon's house. It was largely a matter of finding the right take and syncing it up with John Cooper

Clarke's recording. Simon spent quite a few hours a day or two later experimenting with different colour grades.

How did the experience of working on a short film differ to the feature films you have worked on?

They are a million miles apart. My short had a crew of three, no money and we shot it in a day in my hometown. *Home of the Brave* had a crew of several hundred, cost around $12 million and was shot over a couple of months in both Morocco and the US. In *Chrysanthemums* I was the producer and director – the ultimate responsibility for the entire film was in my hands. I organised the whole shoot: crew, location, equipment, shot list, schedule etc. In *Home of the Brave* I was a second assistant director so I dealt with the cast, call sheets, reports, extras etc and we had an entire crew of professionals working in each department.

For the other big films I worked on – *The Doors* and *Born on the Fourth of July* – I was a runner. Most of my time was spent away from the main action and, whenever I was close to it, I was usually too awestruck to take in anything significant. That said, it was an invaluable experience – some of the first steps of my journey into film.

What did you do with the film once it was completed? Did you have a strategy for distributing the film before you started making it?

No real strategy other than to send it to the Nokia festival. Then I came across Withoutabox.com and realised that there are hundreds of film festivals worldwide, year round. So I sent it to a few more and it was selected at a couple. It became a bit like a drug, I wanted the film to be accepted at as many festivals as possible so I sent it to loads of festivals. But, like all good drugs, it got expensive pretty quick and the more rejections I got the less enthusiastic I felt. I had to become more selective, sending it to festivals that were interested in very short films and/or specifically comedies. Since then it's been selected by 15 film festivals (at the time of writing) in five different countries and has won two awards with two more festivals in the offing.

What has come out of showing it at film festivals etc?

A big part of working as a freelance filmmaker is self-promotion. You've got to get in touch and maintain contact with as many people in the business as you can. Having the film selected for film festivals has turned it into my calling card.

Whenever the film is accepted at another film festival, I email my entire contact list to let them know. It's not considered very English blowing your own trumpet like that, but it has to be done. I try to lighten it up a bit with a couple of jokes. I'm sure most people delete the email straight away... although I hope they at least have a laugh. But it's definitely worked in my favour. I sent one to a production manager who I'd been a runner for in Los Angeles, Brian Frankish. He was curious and said he might be able to get me a job on a film he was working on in Morocco. I immediately checked out flight prices to Marrakesh and told him I'd work for free if he paid for my flight and lodging. I sent him my CV and I think he was impressed with what I'd done since we'd last worked together. He ended up giving me a job as assistant director on a movie with Samuel L Jackson and Fifty Cent. Similarly, I sent emails to a record producer, Steve Weltman, who consequently asked me to direct a music video for one of his clients. Like it or not, self-promotion is the name of the game.

It was at one of the festivals in Clermont-Ferrand, in France, that I met Dawn Sharpless. She's head at Dazzle Films, a short-film distribution company, and has since taken *Chrysanthemums* on. So as well as prestige and continuing work, I also have a distributor thanks to the festival success of the film.

What did you learn from your experiences making *Chrysanthemums the Word*? In retrospect, are there any things that you would have done differently?

I certainly learned that you can't be prepared enough. Storyboards, rehearsals, recces – they're all vital if you can afford the time. But the most important thing I learned as a director is to think about the way you want the piece to look, the meaning behind the shot, what it is you want to say. Anyone can put a camera on a tripod and say 'action', but it's the creativity behind it that's key. I often look back at work that I've done and cringe, thinking 'Surely I could have done better than that'. Uniquely, with *Chrysanthemums* I haven't had that feeling yet. Maybe it's because it's so short. Or because it's done so well on the festival circuit. I suppose it would have been nice to have shot it on HDV for the experience, and maybe I could have added some music, but that might have distracted the audience from the poem. So, on the whole, I would say that I wouldn't have done anything differently.

What did you do after completing *Chrysanthemums the Word*?

I sent the film to Nokia and waited. A couple of months later there was an announcement online of the ten finalists. Sadly, *Chrysanthemums* wasn't one of them. Disappointed, but not overly surprised, I threw away the postal receipt – I'd sent it via the Royal Mail's Special Delivery to ensure it got there. Then I pulled it out of the bin again and called the Royal Mail, just to double-check. They told me they'd lost the DVD package. What?! 'Yeah, a few months ago. Sorry.' Sorry? 'This is my career', I protested, 'not some bloody birthday card!' So they sent me a cheque. For £6.50. I was furious. As a knee-jerk reaction I decided, sod them, I'll send it to a load of other film festivals! In retrospect, of course, this was of no loss to them, quite the opposite. But I couldn't think of anything better.

Since then it's been a resounding success. Recently, the 15-second film festival ran again. I sent them another copy. I was on holiday when the deadline came up, so I called them a week later when I got back to make sure it had arrived. They hadn't received it! Would you believe, the Royal Mail had lost it in the post? Again! I explained to the festival judges that I'd made *Chrysanthemums* over a year ago *especially* for their festival and told them about the whole post office thing. They said, if I can bring it in, by hand, that day, they would consider it for the festival. I took a train into London and 90 minutes later it was in their hands. Next week, as a result, I'm going to the Hammersmith Palais, joining with the likes of Helen Mirren, Ken Loach, James Nesbitt and Stephen Frears to compete for an award at the British Independent Film Awards.

If my filmmaking career goes to pot, I think there's room in the market to set up some competition against the Royal Mail.

What are your plans for the future?

One of the festival prizes I won was 5,000 Euros to go towards the budget of another film, provided generously by itsallelectric.com. We're doing a sequel (also a prequel) to *Chrysanthemums* in which we resolve where the flowers came from. Keeping up the flower theme, we're calling it *Back to the Fuchsia*.

Having made a music video this summer in Los Angeles for solo artist Tara Chinn, I'm hoping in early 2007 to direct another promo for the same record company Zest Music/Greensleeves. They have a Reggae artist Nasio Fontaine, based on the island of Dominica in the Caribbean, where we're hoping to shoot the film.

In the meantime, I'm developing a feature film to be shot in the US. Whatever happens, I plan on continuing working in the film business, at least until the inspiration runs dry.

What advice do you have for filmmakers considering making a short?

Give up, you're insane! Have you seen the competition? You don't stand a chance. It's become a completely flooded market. Go into something worthwhile, something that guarantees an income, something sensible. You're wasting your time. You know, deep down, you're not good enough.

If that puts you off in any way, then take the advice. If it doesn't, you're half way there. Now just do it... but don't trust your film in the hands of the Royal Mail.

What do you enjoy most about making short films?

I love the camaraderie, working with a selected group of mates, cast and crew. I enjoy the process of overcoming obstacles as a team, even if it is sometimes nerve-wracking. And there's a tremendous sense of pleasure and pride in screening the final product in front of the crew, friends and family.

RESOURCES

ACTING UNIONS

www.equity.org.uk
www.sag.org

CASTING RESOURCES

www.spotlight.com
www.sagindie.org
www.freecr.co.uk
www.uk.castingcallpro.com
www.castnet.co.uk
www.ukscreen.com
www.castinguk.com
www.thecastingsuite.com
www.craigslist.org

CREW AND EQUIPMENT AND POST-PRODUCTION DIRECTORIES

www.mandy.com
www.ukscreen.com
www.shootingpeople.org
www.kftv.com

COMPOSITING/EFFECTS SOFTWARE

www.apple.com/shake
www.apple.com/motion
www.adobe.com/products/aftereffects

EDITING SOFTWARE

www.adobe.com
www.apple.com/finalcutpro
www.avid.com
www.dvs.de

FILM COMMISSIONS

www.filmlondon.org.uk
www.ukfilmcouncil.org.uk

GENERAL RESOURCE SITES FOR SHORT FILMMAKERS

www.britfilms.com
www.bfi.org.uk
www.bbc.co.uk/dna/filmnetwork
www.filmmaking.net
www.film-center.com
www.shortfilmchannel.com
www.ukfilm.org
www.pact.co.uk
www.theknowledgeonline.com
www.nypg.com
www.exposure.co.uk
www.dfilm.com
www.freefilmsoftware.co.uk

GRADING

www.redgiantsoftware.com
www.geniusofdavinci.com

MUSIC RIGHTS

www.prs.co.uk
www.musiciansunion.org.uk

PRODUCTION SOFTWARE

www.junglesoftware.com

www.write-brain.com

SCRIPTWRITING SOFTWARE AND RESOURCES

www.screenwriting.com

www.movietools.com

www.finaldraft.com

www.screenplay.com

SOUNDTRACK SOFTWARE

www.digidesign.com

www.apple.com/logicpro

www.apple.com/finalcutstudio/soundtrackpro

SOUND EFFECTS LIBRARIES

www.sound-effects-library.com

www.sonomic.com

www.a1freesoundeffects.com

www.soundeffects.com

www.grsites.com

www.filmsound.org

STORYBOARDING SOFTWARE

www.storyboardartist.com

www.powerproduction.com

SHORT FILMS ONLINE

www.atomfilms.com

www.shortfuzed.com

www.depict.org

www.nokiashorts.com

www1.orange.co.uk/60secondsoffame
www.ifilm.com
www.youtube.com
www.alldaybreakfast.ca
www.pixar.com/shorts
www.newvenue.com
www.channel4.com/film/shortsandclips
www.clipland.com
www.bijoucafe.com

SHORT FILM DISTRIBUTION

www.dazzlefilms.co.uk
www.bigfilmshorts.com
www.onedotzero.com
www.britshorts.com
www.sgrin.co.uk

ONLINE FESTIVAL DISTRIBUTION

www.shortfilmdepot.com
www.reelport.com
www.withoutabox.com

SHORT FILM FESTIVAL LISTINGS

www.filmfestivals.com
www.netribution.co.uk

SELECTION OF INTERNATIONAL SHORT FILM FESTIVALS

Angers Premiers Plans (January)
www.premiersplans.org

Aspen Shortsfest (April)
www.aspenfilm.org

Berlin International Film Festival (February)
www.berlinale.de

Bilbao International Festival of Documentary & Short Films
(November)
www.zinebi.com

Brest European Short Film Festival (November)
www.film-festival.brest.com

Brooklyn International Film Festival (June)
www.wbff.org

Cannes International Film Festival (May)
www.festival-cannes.org

Cardiff Screen Festival (November)
www.cardiffscreenfestival.co.uk

Chicago International Film Festival (October)
www.chicagofilmfestival.com

Cinema Jove International Film Festival (June)
www.cinemajovefilmfest.com

Clermont-Ferrand International Short Film Festival (Jan/Feb)
www.clermont-filmfest.com

Cork International Film Festival (October)
www.corkfilmfest.org

Cracow International Festival of Short Films (May/June)
www.cracowfilmfestival.pl

Edinburgh International Film Festival (August)
www.edfilmfest.org.uk

Encounters International Short Film Festival (November)
www.encounters-festival.org.uk

Filmfest Hamburg (September)
www.filmfesthamburg.de

Flanders International Film Festival (October)
www.filmfestival.be

Flickerfest (January)
www.flickerfest.com

Fluxus – International Film Festival on the Internet
www.fluxusonline.com

Halloween Short Film Festival (January)
www.shortfilms.org.uk

Leuven International Short Film Festival (December)
www.shortfilmfestival.org

Los Angeles International Short Film Festival (September)
www.lashortsfest.com

Mecal International Short Film Festival (September)
www.mecalbcn.org

Melbourne International Film Festival (July/August)
www.melbournefilmfestival.com.au

Oberhausen International Short Film Festival (May)
www.kurzfilmtage.de

Palm Springs International Short Film Festival (August)
www.psfilmfest.org

Raindance Film Festival (October)
www.raindancefilmfestival.org

Resfest (October)
www.resfest.com

Rio de Janeiro International Short Film Festival (Nov/Dec)
www.curtacinema.com.br

Rotterdam International Film Festival (Jan/Feb)
www.filmfestivalrotterdam.com

Rushes Soho Short Film Festival (July/August)
www.rushes.co.uk

São Paulo International Film Festival (Oct/Nov)
www.mostra.org

Short Expression: International Film Festival, Guanajuato (July)
www.expresionencorto.com

Short Shorts Film Festival (June)
www.shortshorts.org

Sundance Film Festival (January)
www.sundance.org

Sydney Film Festival (June)
www.sydneyfilmfestival.org

Tampere International Short Film Festival (March)
www.tamperefilmfestival.fi

The Times BFI London Film Festival (Oct/Nov)
www.lff.org.uk

Toronto Worldwide Short Film Festival (June)
www.worldwideshortfilmfest.com

TCM Classic Shorts Competition (November)
www.tcmonline.co.uk

Uppsala International Short Film Festival (October)
www.shortfilmfestival.com

Venice Film Festival (September)
www.labiennale.org/en/cinema

Vienna Short Film Festival (July)
www.shortfilmcompetition.at

INDEX